TEEN CONFIDENCE REVOLUTION

A GUIDE TO CRUSH NEGATIVITY, BOOST SELF-ESTEEM, REDUCE STRESS, AND SLAY YOUR GOALS!

TEEN POWERHOUSE SOCIETY

© **Copyright 2024 - All rights reserved**

The content contained within this book may not be reproduced, duplicated or transmitted without direct written permission from the author or the publisher.

Under no circumstances will any blame or legal responsibility be held against the publisher, or author, for any damages, reparation, or monetary loss due to the information contained within this book, either directly or indirectly.

Legal Notice:

This book is copyright protected. It is only for personal use. You cannot amend, distribute, sell, use, quote or paraphrase any part, or the content within this book, without the consent of the author or publisher.

Disclaimer Notice:

Please note the information contained within this document is for educational and entertainment purposes only. All effort has been executed to present accurate, up to date, reliable, complete information. No warranties of any kind are declared or implied. Readers acknowledge that the author is not engaged in the rendering of legal, financial, medical or professional advice. The content within this book has been derived from various sources. Please consult a licensed professional before attempting any techniques outlined in this book. By reading this document, the reader agrees that under no circumstances is the author responsible for any losses, direct or indirect, that are incurred as a result of the use of the information contained within this document, including, but not limited to, errors, omissions, or inaccuracies.

DEAR AMAZING REVOLUTIONARIES!

Exciting news! Our latest book, Teen Confidence Revolution is your go-to guide for boosting teen confidence. We've poured our hearts into creating a resource that speaks directly to teens *and* parents, offering valuable insights and practical strategies.

Take your journey to the next level with the "Teen Confidence Revolution Workbook." It's a hands-on tool designed to complement the book, turning insights into actionable steps. We believe that the workbook will enhance your experience and make the journey towards confidence more interactive.

It's not required but consider adding the workbook with activities for a deeper, more personal dive into your journey of self-discovery. Thank you for joining the Teen Confidence Revolution!

Warm regards,

Teen Powerhouse Society

DEDICATION

To our beloved students. You have been the heartbeat of our days. From the tentative steps of ninth grade to the confident strides of twelfth, we have walked hand in hand. Weaving together threads of learning, laughter, and love. Your journey of self-discovery has been the greatest privilege to witness.

In your presence, we've found days of inspiration, frustration, gratitude, humor, and above all love. You have been our teachers, as much as we have been yours, and for that, we are endlessly grateful.

As you step into the vast expanse of the world beyond the walls of the classroom, our deepest wish is for you to carry the essence of your unique magic with you. May you be happy, not just in fleeting moments, but in the quiet spaces between. May you be successful, not just in the eyes of the world, but in the whispers of your own heart. And, most importantly, may you be whole human beings, for your completeness is what will heal the world.

CONTENTS

Teen Confidence Revolution	9
1. MAIN CHARACTER ERA: THE SELF-DISCOVERY QUEST	15
Chloe's Story of Self-Awareness	15
Finding Your True North: Who Are You?	17
Discover Your Authenticity	22
Engaging in Self-Expression Through Truthful Communication	26
The Power of Self-Awareness	28
Practice Tool: Keeping a Journal	31
In Summary	32
2. LET YOUR FREAK FLAG FLY: BREAKING FREE FROM THE COMPARISON TRAP	33
A Story of Embracing Uniqueness	33
How to Escape the Pressures of Social Media	36
Embrace Your Uniqueness	40
Cultivating Self-Compassion	42
Practical Tool: Affirmations	44
In Summary	47
3. SLAY BAE! UNLEASHING YOUR INNER CONFIDENCE	49
The Confidence Conundrum	49
What Is Confidence?	51
But the Voices In My Head…All About Positive Self-Talk	58
Confidence-Boosting Strategies	60
Parents/Teachers: How to Help Your Teen Develop Self-Consciousness	62
Practical Tool: Confidence-Building Exercises	63
In Summary	65

4. NOT TODAY, BRUH! TAMING THE STRESS
   MONSTER   67
   Dealing With Academic Pressure   67
   Understanding Stress   69
   Parents/Teachers: How to Recognize Depression   77
   How You Can Beat Stress as a Teen   80
   Parents/Teachers: How to Help Your Teen
   Overcome Stress   84
   In Summary   85

5. TIME TO GET YASSIFIED! GOAL SETTING FOR
   TEENS: DREAM BIG, ACHIEVE BIGGER   89
   The Inspiring Story of Luna Frank, a college
   junior   89
   What Is Goal Setting?   90
   Goal-Setting Theories and Tools   92
   Goal-Setting Tips   99
   Parents/Teachers: How To Support Your Teen's
   Goals   101
   Practical Tool: Choose One of the Tools Below   103
   In Summary   105

6. BE BAD AND BOUJEE: OVERCOMING
   OBSTACLES AND RESILIENCE   107
   A Story of Teen Resilience: Aziza, a Young
   Volunteer in Ghana   107
   Challenges as Opportunities   108
   Obstacles to Embracing Challenges   110
   Building Resilience: Strategies for Success   111
   The Link Between a Growth Mindset and Greater
   Resilience   113
   In Summary   122

7. CREATING A CONFIDENCE REVOLUTION
   COMMUNITY: YOUR SUPPORT NETWORK   123
   Two Sisters Harness the Power of Community   123
   The Power of Connection   124
   Create Your Teen Confidence Revolution
   Community   129
   In Summary   132

8. UNLEASH THE BADDIE: UNLOCK YOUR
   PASSIONS AND DREAMS   135
   A Story of Teen Dreamers   135
   What Is Passion, and How Is It Significant?   136
   Encouraging Your Creative Side   141
   In Summary   146

9. CLAPBACK ON THOSE FEARS: FACING FEARS
   AND OVERCOMING INSECURITIES   147
   Teen Story of Courage   147
   Understanding Your Fears and Insecurities   148
   Confronting Fear Head-On   153
   In Summary   159

   Conclusion   161
   References   165

TEEN CONFIDENCE REVOLUTION

The Teen Confidence Revolution is real. It has transformed the lives of countless teens just like you. If you allow it, it can do the same for you. But, what is confidence? And *why* is it so elusive? We naturally admire confident people, but have you ever wondered why? Why is confidence one of the most sought-after and esteemed personality traits? The answer to these questions can help you understand the deeper reasons that have motivated you to read this book.

Self-confidence is that feeling you get when you're fully assured of who you are, what you can do, and the decisions you make. Signs of self-confidence include believing in yourself and having unwavering faith in your personal characteristics and that you can accomplish anything you set your mind to.

Confident people emanate positivity, thanks to their can-do mindset. At the core of their confidence is a high sense of self-worth and self-respect, also known as self-esteem. In a world where most people—about 85% of the world's population—suffer from low self-esteem, it's no wonder why confidence stands out (Self Esteem School, n.d.).

There is a deep sense of peace that comes with being self-confident. Anywhere you go, whatever happens, you're relaxed because you believe you can handle whatever life throws your way and it will be alright. Your positivity comes from knowing you've got what it takes to tackle anything. As a confident person, you'll naturally assert power and sound knowledgeable. People will want to listen when you speak because it will be clear that you believe in what you have to say.

Set your confidence revolution in motion today by acknowledging that change starts with you. Reject the idea that low confidence is a part of who you are and that you must be born with confidence. Embrace ALL of you: your mistakes, where you're lacking right now, and the blunders you might make in the future.

Revolutions are etched in history because through blood, sweat, and tears they have the capacity to transform a dream into reality. Similarly, through hard work, consistency, and determination, you can overcome your insecurities, and low self-esteem and increase your confidence to reach your full potential.

Imagine your confidence revolution like a total makeover in how you usually think or act—but all for the better! It's that moment when you decide you want the freedom to be your true self. You're rebelling against your old ways and pushing yourself to build new habits. Trust me, it's not a walk in the park, and that's what makes it revolutionary!

Your confidence revolution starts with firmly believing that you can learn to be confident and commit to working towards that goal. If you are ready to break free from self-doubt, low self-esteem, and negativity to finally pursue your goals, express yourself, and interact with others, this book is for you. Envision a more confident you, one who is no longer held back by crippling self-doubt and insecurities, and read on. You will learn how to effectively manage the stress that comes from your social life, academics, emotions, and the general complexities of modern life, and embark on a personal self-development journey.

Use this book as your guide and implement the various tools as you go along, read some inspirational stories from other teens, and use proven strategies to help you reach your goals. At the beginning of your journey, we'll explore the idea of self-discovery, address the role of social media and harmful comparisons, and learn more about the building blocks of self-confidence. Later on, we'll discuss effective stress management and goal-setting techniques, the resilience required to overcome challenges that stand in your way, and how best to garner support from your friends and family.

It's important to emphasize that, although this journey is a personal revolution where you'll be working on building your confidence, having a community to support you is equally vital. Relying on those you trust the most can provide the encouragement you need, especially during challenging times. Our advice is to read this book alongside a parent, trusted teacher, friend or coach. You are not alone in this transformation.

In the last leg of our journey, we'll give you the tools to discover your dreams and passions, tackle your fears and insecurities, and celebrate your progress. Change is seldom easy. Despite the challenges it poses, change is often necessary, especially for a teen standing at the gateway to adulthood. The decisions you make now will have far-reaching effects. Commit to becoming more confident today, and enjoy the benefits throughout the rest of your life.

Real-life success stories not only motivate us but they provide much-needed evidence that change and success are possible. You'll find that most people who share their success stories are rather ordinary, with no superpower or exceptional talent. The only notable thing that sets them apart is their consistent determination and commitment to self-development and improvement. If they can do it, so can you.

Read Olivia's story below and learn how she overcame the challenges she faced growing up in an unstable home to become a high school graduate with a strong sense of self-awareness, a clear vision for her future, and admirable long-term goals.

Olivia's parents moved their family around a lot. Due to this, she and her siblings often missed school in between moves. Eventually, Olivia developed a strong dislike for school, because she constantly felt overwhelmed from falling behind in her academics and always being the 'new kid' in school. Although Olivia's family lacked a stable address, the kind of neighborhoods they lived in were consistent: poor and crime-ridden.

Olivia would hardly spend any time at home, preferring to stay out, as she puts it in her own words, "I really didn't like going home after school, so I'd always find something to do or someone to hang with to keep me out until late." Olivia was trying to avoid facing the grim confines of her living situation. After intercepting a serious conflict at their latest home, the police arrested both of Olivia's parents.

Child Protection Services got involved and soon Olivia found herself placed at a local center and sanctuary for children who suffer from abuse and neglect and engage in risky behaviors. She was skeptical at first, unsure if the place could actually help her. Her counselor, who worked with her every day from the moment she arrived, says, "When Olivia started, she was so unsure of who she was and you could easily see in the way she interacted with others that she had low self-esteem."

As part of the program at the center, Olivia took part in group activities, attended therapy, learned life skills, and attended school every day. As Olivia tells it, "Once I started the program, I realized that I really like to learn. Before, I always felt like learning was a chore but now I can't get enough of it. I love learning new facts about the world, and figuring out how things work." Olivia's positive attitude and determination were so powerful that she rose above all her initial doubts and negativity to become the leader of her dormitory.

After graduating high school, Olivia interned at the center's annual summer camp and found another way to use her leadership skills. Today Olivia's goal is to obtain a degree in social work, and she has set her sights on giving back to the community by helping children in need to rise above their difficult circumstances. By the strength of her will and the clarity of her vision, she can have every reason to believe she will succeed.

Like Olivia, you can identify as self-driven, community-focused, and socially conscious, even if you don't feel fully prepared. Have faith that with time, your confidence will grow. Today, vow to take the courageous first steps to be better and to do better. When you embrace your own confidence revolution you revolt against self-doubt, negative habits, and insecurities. This revolution is about committing to creating new, positive habits that will benefit you and those around you.

Once you acknowledge that change begins with you, you'll realize that your actions (or inactions) today can influence your future success, happiness, and well-being. The duty of self-improvement rests on your shoulders just as much today, as it always will for the rest of your life. Take a stand and commit to personal growth and future today.

Change may not always be easy, but it's necessary for your journey into adulthood. The confidence revolution is your opportunity for personal growth and transformation, and it all starts with you. Let's begin!

1

MAIN CHARACTER ERA: THE SELF-DISCOVERY QUEST

> *Knowing yourself is the beginning of all wisdom.*
>
> — ARISTOTLE

Don't you think the idea of getting to know yourself is a bit ironic? You are the person you spend the most time with. You've been in your own company since the day you were born, never spending a moment apart. Yet, astonishingly, parts of your identity still remain obscure to you. To reach your full potential, you must prioritize self-discovery.

CHLOE'S STORY OF SELF-AWARENESS

When Chloe, a seventeen-year-old high school student, began seeing a life coach, she was unaware of how her negative self-talk was affecting her mindset and holding her back from trying new things. This lack of self-awareness caused her to suffer from self-doubt, feeling inadequate, and a crippling fear of rejection and failure.

Negative self-talk came so naturally to Chloe that she wasn't even aware she was doing it. The negative way in which she was always speaking to herself held her back from taking the risk she'd always wanted to take—auditioning for her school musical. She was afraid of taking the shot because she told herself she was going to fail.

With the help of her life coach, Chloe became aware of her negative self-talk and how it was destroying her confidence. After becoming more self-aware, Chloe was able to stop her negative self-talk and begin practicing positive affirmations instead.

With these new skills, she was able to muster the courage to step out of her comfort zone and audition for a role in the musical. While her nervousness never disappeared, Chloe practiced every day and gave her best performance. After the audition, she went running to her life coach's office, barely able to contain her excitement as she shared how positive self-talk helped her get the part.

When Chloe began consistently telling herself, "I can take on challenges, I am a smart person who can figure things out," she gave herself wings to fly. Before she knew it, her new affirmation practice had her flying over all the obstacles that she set up in her own mind through negativity.

Similarly, by reading this book and applying what you'll learn, you too can overcome your fears, become more self-aware, and achieve what you never thought possible.

FINDING YOUR TRUE NORTH: WHO ARE YOU?

Self-discovery is a journey that often begins in early adolescence and extends well throughout the rest of your life. As you advance through different life stages and experience more of life, your perceptions, maturity, and purpose change. Your identity is something that tends to be dynamic, making self-discovery an ongoing process.

Early Adolescence (10-13)

In this stage, your brain and body are changing due to the onset of puberty. While witnessing your body grow and change may be an interesting experience, it can also be stressful when you think about how these changes will affect other aspects of your life.

During early adolescence, you may have an increased need for privacy and start feeling more self-conscious. You begin to define yourself outside the context of your family life. In this age bracket, you'll typically have a black-and-white perception of life, where things are always right or wrong, with no in-betweens. As your sensitivity to feedback heightens, you'll attach more importance to fitting in with your peers.

You may enter into a state of *identity moratorium* in this phase, which often continues through to late adolescence. An identity moratorium is a state where teens are actively exploring their identity without firmly committing to any specific choices. This includes trying out different looks, hairstyles, and fashion, hanging out with new friends, and experimenting with new hobbies.

You might be thinking:

"Why are my breasts growing slower than my friend's?"

"My mom never remembers to knock on my door before barging in!"

"I've had this haircut for ages, I think I want to try something new"

Middle Adolescence (14-17)

In this phase, the identity moratorium continues. However, you can now take a firmer stance on ethical or moral issues that you believe in.

As a teen in this phase, you'll start considering your beliefs in context of other people's worldviews. You'll start to see your religion, race, or culture in light of how they're perceived by others around you and by the world at large. You begin to define who you are in the context of society and where you fit into it.

You might be thinking:

"I need to speak to my neighbor about keeping his dog tied to a tree all day. That's wrong!"

"I'm a black boy but I'm not a criminal. It's disappointing that some people will assume that I am."

"I wonder how my food choices affect my health and the world around me. What if I became vegan?"

Late Adolescence (18-24)

This stage begins after high school and extends throughout college. In this phase, you'll begin to define who you are in terms of your intimate relationships. You'll begin to develop strong commitments to your beliefs, such as religion or political views.

By this stage, you already have some experience of the world away from your sheltered home environment. Your views and aspirations are likely to change in accordance with your new perception of reality. You start to focus more on the future, taking action and making decisions to attain your long-term goals. You're beginning to identify and establish your core values, and as a result, you also develop stronger friendships and romantic relationships.

The relationship you share with your parents will change and you begin to perceive your parents more as equals. You'll seek their opinions and advice with respect, but will not take what they say as an order. In this way, you automatically assert your autonomy from your parents, as you increasingly become emotionally and physically separated from them.

By now, the identity moratorium should be nearing its end as you reach the stage of commitment. The commitment stage occurs after you've experimented with different personas and have decided which one suits you best.

What you might be thinking:

"I really want to start a side hustle but let me ask my dad what he thinks before I decide."

"She likes me but I'm a Christian and she's an Atheist. How will we connect through our faiths? It won't work."

"I've always been fascinated with space, but I realize now that I'd rather pursue a career in Mathematics"

How To Navigate Your Journey Toward Self-Discovery

- Acknowledge your strengths. A good way to learn what you enjoy doing is by making a list of your strengths. Your list can give you valuable insight into understanding your passions.
- Determine your worldview. How do you see the world, with all its beauty, diversity, events, threats, and problems? Are you in favor of wisdom, justice, or generosity? Everyone sees things differently and the lens through which you see the world provides insights into your identity.
- Determine your goals. Your goals forecast the kind of life you'd like to live in the future and they indicate where your passions lie. Staying committed to your goals helps you pave the way to a fulfilling and purpose-driven life.

- Identify your core values. The ideals and principles that you take a firm stand on showing you what you value. Do you value equity, honesty, compassion, and respect for life? Values offer key insights into your developing identity.

Parents/Teachers: Helping Your Teen Through Their Journey of Self-Discovery

Demonstrate the Practice of Self-Reflection

Teens tend to make quick and often impulsive decisions. As a parent, show them that the best decisions are made by taking a moment to slow down and think carefully. Practice thoughtfulness in your decision-making, actions, and the words you say. A great way to include your teen in this process is to ask them for their input when making a decision.

Show That It's Okay to Learn Slowly

Many teens experience tremendous pressure when they believe that they have a limited window of time in which to discover who they are and decide on what they want from their future. Show them that even at your age, self-discovery still happens and there is always an opportunity to decide who you are and what you want to do with your life. The answers to these pivotal questions will come in time and they do not need to stress about not having all the answers. Assure them that self-discovery and identity-building is a lifelong process.

Illustrate the Enjoyable Aspects of Adulthood

As a parent or caregiver, your teen looks to you for an idea of what they can expect from adulthood. Make an effort to maintain your social life, set aside time to spend with your family, go to fun places, and engage in your hobbies. Teens should know that there is more to adulthood than working long hours and worrying about bills.

Show You Can Be Spontaneous

You want your teen to believe that there will be room for spontaneity well into adulthood. They shouldn't feel rushed to 'try everything they ever wanted to while they still can'. For example, on an ordinary Wednesday night, say "Let's go to the beach for a quick dip."

Be a Lighthouse Parent

A lighthouse is a timeless symbol of safety and stability, providing guidance from a distance. Adolescence is a stage where your teen should be allowed to explore different forms of self-expression. They should feel that you trust them to make their own decisions and learn from their own mistakes. By being a lighthouse parent, your teen will know that your presence and support are guaranteed, but still feel free to grow.

DISCOVER YOUR AUTHENTICITY

Authenticity is the quality of being genuine, and true to your own character, beliefs, and values, without any pretense or imitation. It involves being honest and transparent in your actions, thoughts, and expressions, and not trying to conform under pressure or to the expectations of others.

Being authentic means having a deep sense of self-awareness and a commitment to living in alignment with your true identity and principles. Authenticity often leads to more meaningful and fulfilling relationships, as it fosters trust and a sense of connection with others who appreciate and accept you for who you are.

The Benefits of Being Authentic

Less Stress and Anxiety

When you are pretending to be someone you're not, you're like an actor who stays in character 24/7. It can be exhausting because, unlike real actors, you won't hear a "Cut!" at the end of every scene. Pretending to be someone else can cause you unnecessary stress and anxiety because you'll always be worried your performance will fall short.

More Satisfying Friendships

When you are authentic you will attract people who understand and appreciate the real you. When you are around such people, you won't feel like you have to hide parts of yourself or pretend to be different from your real self. Your relationships will be a source of fun with no pressure.

Increases Self-Confidence

When you are comfortable in your own skin and can fearlessly and unapologetically be your true self, you exude unshakable confidence. Believing that you can be yourself and still enjoy a full social life, achieve your goals, and be happy is the epitome of self-confidence.

How to Be Authentic

Find Out What It Is You're Trying to Suppress

When you're wearing a mask to hide your authentic self and project a different persona, you're effectively hiding certain parts of yourself. What aspects of yourself do you wish to keep hidden, and what are the reasons behind wanting to hide this information from others?

Is it an interest you think others find strange? Or your unique perspective on life? Is it a weakness? Once you uncover what you're hiding, you can take it apart and work on it.

Speak Your Truth

Commit to expressing your true thoughts, feelings, ideas, and beliefs. When you would otherwise remain silent, speak up. Express your authenticity fearlessly, but respectfully, and apologize to no one.

Make Peace With the Fact That You Can't Please Everyone

People-pleasers are those who constantly choose to bear the responsibility of fulfilling other people's needs and expectations. The need to make others happy to gain their approval or validation is one of the major obstacles to authenticity. One way to break free from the desire to please people is to stop taking feedback personally. Instead, view feedback as a reflection of the person giving it, and not of who you are.

Identify Your Values to Enhance Your Authenticity

Values are deeply held beliefs, principles, and priorities that guide and shape your thoughts, behaviors, and decision-making processes. Your values represent what you consider to be important, meaningful, and worth pursuing.

Having firmly established values will give you a certain degree of consistency in how you manage challenges that come your way. If you hold integrity as a value, your approach to situations requiring a choice between honesty and dishonesty will align consistently with this core value.

We can only commit to values that speak to us on a deeper level. Nobody can decide your values for you. For inspiration, see the list of fifteen values below with brief descriptions. Which of them resonates with you?

- Accountability: Taking responsibility for one's actions.
- Charity: Helping and giving to those in need.
- Diversity: Embracing different people and perspectives.
- Freedom: The power to act without limitations.
- Fun: Enjoyable and amusing activities.
- Humility: Absence of pride or arrogance.
- Integrity: Firm commitment to moral principles and honesty.
- Justice: Upholding moral conduct and fairness.

- Kindness: Showing benevolence, consideration, and helpfulness.
- Tolerance: Fair and permissive attitude toward differing opinions and beliefs.
- Loyalty: Staying faithful to commitments and obligations.
- Tradition: Inherited or customary patterns of thought and behavior.
- Health: Physical, mental, and emotional well-being, by eating healthy and exercising regularly.

ENGAGING IN SELF-EXPRESSION THROUGH TRUTHFUL COMMUNICATION

How authentic you are depends on how truthfully you communicate with others in both verbal and nonverbal ways. Are the nonverbal cues you give to others in agreement with what you feel inside? Do you smile when you're really feeling uncomfortable? Do you say "Alright, I'll do it" when you can't? Truthful communication is expressing your genuine feelings and emotions to others, which leads to authentic self-expression.

Self-expression is a means through which individuals express their inner thoughts and emotions to the outside world, often using various forms of communication, such as art, writing, speaking, fashion, or other creative outlets. When you embrace authenticity, your self-expression becomes more aligned with your personality and identity, helping you to comfortably display on the outside, the way you feel on the inside.

Tips to Help You Engage in Truthful Communication

Have Empathy

Imagine your friend asks you for your help with a school project that's due soon. They're overwhelmed. However, you've got an important math test the next day, and you need to study. With empathy, you say "I can see you're stressed, and I'd love to help, but I have a big math test tomorrow that I really need to study for. I know it's tough to hear, and I'm sorry about that. Is there any other way I can assist you or support you through this project?" In this way, you're communicating truthfully while letting them know you understand their situation and how they must be feeling.

Be Consistent

Being consistent means doing what you say you'll do. It is like keeping your promises, to yourself and others. Imagine you promised your little brother or sister that you'd play with them after school. However, at the end of the school day, your new friend invites you to play video games at their house. A few other cool kids from your class are going too. You feel honored to have even been invited but being consistent means politely turning down the invitation to honor the promise you made to your sibling.

Be Direct and Use Facts

Being direct means getting straight to the point. Imagine you borrowed your friend's book and accidentally spilled juice on it. You could say, "I'm really sorry, but I spilled juice on your book." That's being direct because you're not making excuses or avoiding the problem. You're just saying what happened.

THE POWER OF SELF-AWARENESS

Self-awareness is the conscious knowledge and understanding of your own thoughts, feelings, behaviors, strengths, weaknesses, values, and beliefs. It involves your capacity for self-examination, and the ability to recognize yourself as an individual separate from your environment and other people.

Why Is Self-Awareness Important for Teens?

As an adolescent, it's important to understand that developing self-awareness is a crucial part of your transition from childhood to adulthood. It serves as a foundation for your academic success, future career productivity, self-management, goal setting, career selection, stress management, and understanding relationships. Your self-awareness will help you recognize how your identity influences the perceptions and reactions of others, enabling you to adapt your communication style to respond to the needs of those you interact with, which fosters stronger relationships.

Hone Your Self-Awareness

Try Mindful Meditation

One of the reasons why we may lack self-awareness is because we overthink. We allow our thoughts to run free unchecked, leading us to believe that we are our thoughts. Meditation means simply relaxing and focusing fully on your breathing. Keep your concentration purely on the air entering and leaving your lungs. When you catch your mind wandering, bring it back to focus. With time, you'll become more aware of your thought processes and begin to detach your identity from them.

Try Journaling (Yes, it Works)

There is no right or wrong way to journal. Simply write whatever's going on in your head at the moment. You can write anything, from thoughts, hopes, fears, exciting events, and goals to future plans, to name a few. Your past journal entries will be like a special window into your state of mind at the time. It's also a great way to reflect and see how much you've changed and grown.

Document Your Plans and Future Goals

Your goals and plans are clear indicators of your desires and motives. Self-consciousness is about being aware of what motivates you, what you believe is worth striving for, and what you're ready to sacrifice to get it. You can do this in your journal, in a special section, or on a piece of paper and stick it on your wall.

Be Attuned to Your Feelings

Feelings are a major part of us. Being self-aware has a lot to do with your ability to pay attention to your emotions and their triggers. Ask yourself, "What am I feeling now? and "Why do I feel this way?" The answers to these questions will help you understand how to cope with people or things that irritate you.

Step Out of Your Comfort Zone

Your comfort zone is where you behave almost on autopilot; it's the place where you don't expect any surprises and is the place where you feel most comfortable. When you dare to put yourself in unfamiliar situations and observe your responses, you'll gain a wealth of information about who you are, like discovering your dreams, passions, and important values. You can start with small things like talking to new people at school, trying out a new sport, or changing your regular hangout spot.

Parents/Teachers: Help Your Teen Develop Self-Awareness

Encourage Teens to Identify and Express Emotions

Many teens do not share all their thoughts and emotions with their parents. If your teen doesn't open up to you, have a conversation with them about safe ways to express themselves.

Model Self-Awareness

One way you could model self-awareness is by sharing your feelings with your teen. Sharing your emotions shows that you are aware of them, how they affect you, and what triggers them.

Talk About the Use of Labels

Refrain from referring to your teen (or anybody else) by using labels. It's important to negate the idea that people can be defined by one aspect of their personalities. It can be quite frustrating for teens who are working towards figuring out their identities to be predefined based on stereotypes or prejudices.

Discuss Their Strengths

We tend to be our own worst critics. During this time of self-discovery, your teen may be trying to grasp their own identity by comparing themselves to others. It's common for teens to develop low self-esteem, and low confidence when they idealize someone else's talents, qualities, and looks that are different from their own. Help your teen acknowledge their own strengths so they gain a positive self-image and strong self-confidence.

PRACTICE TOOL: KEEPING A JOURNAL

Keeping a journal has many benefits. Many great stories we know today come from the journals of those who came before us. Some of the most famous journal keepers are Anne Frank, Lena Mukhina, Marie Curie, and Charles Darwin. A journal can serve as a collection of memories, a method of self-care, and a safe place for self-expression. Moreover, the more you write, the better you'll become at articulating your thoughts and feelings.

Journaling techniques

- Dialogue: Write as if you're having a conversation with someone, like a friend.
- Free flow: For up to five minutes, put your pen to paper and write/draw/doodle nonstop.
- Listicle: If you have a list of things you want to write about, but want to be very brief, this is a good option.

- Write a poem: Write poems or lyrics or play with words.
- Use drawings: You can draw cartoon characters to embody the feelings you want to express.

IN SUMMARY

This has been an in-depth chapter where we've explored the broad topic of self-discovery and we unpacked the complex concepts of authenticity and self-awareness. Lastly, you have learned about the powerful tool of journaling as a way for you to document your journey as you grow to experience more confidence and success, through your teen years and beyond. The next chapter will build on what we've covered here, with the topic of breaking free from social comparisons.

2

LET YOUR FREAK FLAG FLY: BREAKING FREE FROM THE COMPARISON TRAP

> *When you embrace your difference, your DNA, your look or heritage or religion or your unusual name, that's when you start to shine.*
>
> — BETHANY FRANKEL

A STORY OF EMBRACING UNIQUENESS

Felix Goldberg was born with a congenital heart disease, and had to undergo a lot of medical treatment as a child. As a teen, Felix viewed this as a weakness, a shame he couldn't bear to reveal. He feared the misunderstanding and judgment that might come with telling everyone that he had a heart that wasn't the same as everyone else's. Throughout high school, he harbored this fear.

However, as he became more assured of who he was, he realized that how he saw himself was more important than how he thought others saw him. Felix began to experience the power of his thoughts and started to view his disorder as a strength, as something that made him unique. Now an adult, Felix's positive attitude towards his condition has allowed him to accept himself fully. Because of this, he radiates authenticity and confidence and hopes it will inspire others to embrace their uniqueness.

The Social Media Illusion

Obsessive Compulsive Scrolling

Social media companies have become experts at how to keep you scrolling. The more people engage with their content, the more money these companies make. Have you ever wondered what methods these social media platforms use to keep your mind stuck in 'scroll' mode? Why do we slip into an almost hypnotic state, unaware of the time slipping by, as we mindlessly consume an endless supply of content?

One of the contributing factors is personalized content. Your Instagram experience is unique as all the content that is presented to you, in terms of posts, suggestions, and ads that are tailored to match your interests. Social media platforms collect information about the topics you search for, the accounts you follow, the content you view most, and the topics you engage with. Using this information, they program their algorithms to present you with content that best matches your past activities.

If you're an Instagram-using fitness enthusiast, you'll probably spend a lot of time on the platform engaging with fitness content, following fitness influencers, searching for fitness gear, or creating fitness-related posts on your own page. Instagram then uses this information to present you with fitness-related ads on the app, and other relevant content.

As you scroll down you see content you enjoy and you wonder what else there is, so you scroll down some more. As you know, the content is never-ending and you could potentially spend a significant amount of your day scrolling.

In 2018, the Pew Research Center reported that 43% of teens aged 13-17 felt compelled to post content on social media to appear favorable to their audience, while 37% also felt pressured to maximize likes and comments. These statistics give you an idea of how successful social media platforms have become in taking a significant bite out of your day.

The Cycle of Negative Feedback

The cycle of negative feedback begins when you attach your self-worth to how other people react to you on social media. The cycle occurs when positive feedback (comments and likes) causes your self-esteem to rise and negative feedback (no likes or comments, or negative comments) causes it to plummet.

Consider the following scenario:

You prep your surroundings, placing everything strategically. You then choose the perfect angle, with just enough light. Satisfied with the background, you take close to a hundred selfies, only to find one worthy of posting—just barely. You then spend close to an hour editing the picture. Trying out dozens of filters, effects, and tools to perfect an image that was already perfect because you were in it.

Armed with the perfect picture, you proceed to write a suitably perfect caption. Because what's a selfie without a killer caption, right? After countless drafts (and perhaps help from ChatGPT) you finally get a caption that's a perfect blend: evocative, intelligent, and humorous.

You post the picture and the caption and wait for the likes and comments. The next day, still nothing. You eventually decide that even negative feedback would've been better than no feedback. You feel crushed and wonder why you didn't get any attention. The negative feelings start swirling and your confidence takes a nosedive.

HOW TO ESCAPE THE PRESSURES OF SOCIAL MEDIA

Go Offline

Being offline always makes you wonder what you're missing. Who's doing what right now? Where are your classmates hanging out over the weekend? What did your friends or favorite influencer post today? All these questions seem important to you because of FOMO (fear of missing out). Nobody wants to be lost when someone from their class asks them "Did you see what so and so posted last night? You're so delayed, it was LIT!" But there's more to life than staying updated on what's happening in other people's lives.

Would you rather be having fun, doing stuff, meeting people, and learning new things, or idly scrolling through the memories of *other* people's life experiences? It might be time to do a social media challenge of a different kind: Going on a week-long social media break. During that week only use your phone for texts and calls. After a week without social media, you'll realize your life really doesn't have to revolve around it.

Be Mindful

Heighten your awareness of how social media is affecting your mental, emotional, and physical health. Does your confidence or self-esteem depend on the attention you get online? By becoming more aware of the nature and extent of the influence social media has on your feelings, motivation, and overall well-being, you'll be better able to practice healthy social media habits that promote your well-being.

If you notice that an influencer whose life you admire tends to shame and make fun of people who are not at their best, unfollow them. Rather fill your screen with content that encourages positivity and motivation and not otherwise.

Parents/Teachers: How to Help Your Teen Break Free From The Pressures of Social Media

Don't Belittle the Role of Social Media in Your Teen's Life

The number one mistake you can make when talking to your teen about social media is downplaying its importance in their lives. Your teen will automatically dismiss whatever you have to say because they'll assume that you don't understand the way things are in their world. Your teen won't be able to help but view your advice as irrelevant and impractical.

Teens today don't know any other life, other than one that seamlessly intertwines reality and the virtual world. To them, something that happened online, might as well have happened right before their eyes. So, the first step is to acknowledge and accept that social media may be an indispensable part of your teen's life. Let this be the bedrock of all other interventions.

Help Your Teen to Connect With the Real World

In the past, it was virtually impossible to escape your reality. People lived in the moment and had a relative grasp of what was going on around them. Today, it's possible to fully immerse yourself in a virtual world that exists parallel to reality. In this online world, *likes* serve as the currency, *followers* are cherished communities, and *comments* are the means of communication. So, don't assume being mindful of reality comes naturally to your teen.

Encourage your teen to spend face-to-face time with their friends. Let them go to the mall, or movies, or have lunch somewhere. If you can, take your family on a social-media-free vacation. It doesn't have to be expensive, maybe a week-long camping trip in the woods. Ban all electronics at the dinner table or during family barbecues or any other family time. If you have Wi-Fi at home, consider turning it off after a certain time, say 9:30 p.m.

Encourage Them to View Social Media Images With a Critical Eye

Tell your teen that most people practice selective posting, where they only post images and videos that shine a positive light on their relationships, friendships, financial status, physical appearance, and lifestyle in general. This means that to the person viewing their page, their lives might seem like the epitome of success, happiness, beauty, and perfection—even though this is often not the case.

Help your teen understand that, when someone posts that they got their degree, they often won't post that they also failed a few exams to earn it. A picture of a guy with a flashy new car won't reveal the debt he incurred to get it. When a girl posts a picture of her and her boyfriend on a romantic dinner date, she won't post that he'd been unfaithful in the past. People always post the positive aspects of their lives, but just because they don't reveal their difficulties, challenges, or imperfections, doesn't mean they don't have any.

Help your teen to realize that just like they have plenty of ups and downs in their lives, so do other people as well. Highlight that ultimately what's most important in life is getting up each time you fall, as it builds resilience and overall confidence.

EMBRACE YOUR UNIQUENESS

You are unique and you can never be replaced. There is no duplicate of you, nor will there ever be. Your thoughts and actions are truly one-of-a-kind. Take a moment to stand in front of a mirror, closely examine yourself, smile, and breathe. You'll notice how distinct and special you are. No one can read you or predict your actions because your identity defies any simple definition. You are beyond any categorization or simplified description.

The Importance of Uniqueness

Imagine the world as an expansive orchestra, producing harmonious music. In this grand ensemble, every individual plays a vital role by contributing their unique instruments and sounds. Neglecting to play one's part disrupts the entire symphony. Your uniqueness is your precious contribution to the majestic orchestra that is our world.

Think of all the important roles people play in our society. Social workers advocate the well-being of the underprivileged, teachers who help students acquire knowledge, and doctors who work long hours to help us when we're sick. If not for uniqueness, we wouldn't have a well-functioning society.

Being unique means allowing others a peek into what's inside of you as well. It means sharing your values, goals, thoughts, beliefs, and identity with others. When people catch a glimpse of your uniqueness, they will want more of it. Allow others to be intrigued by you. Being unique allows you to attract other equally unique people who might have similar values, goals, and beliefs. By being your unique self you will attract people who want to be a part of your life.

How Can You Embrace Your Uniqueness?

Notice how this section is not titled 'How can you *be* unique'. The truth is that you were born unique, just like every human being alive today. From time to time, we need to regain mindfulness to reconnect with our identity and remember and embrace our uniqueness. This is how you let your freak flag fly.

Don't Fear the Unbeaten Path

"Do not go where the path may lead, go instead where there is no path and leave a trail," said Ralph Waldo Emerson. The fear of walking alone will make you a follower for life. Stop being afraid to stand out. When you walk your own path, even when you are afraid, you radiate confidence. Having confidence means knowing that you'll be okay with some people not understanding or accepting you because there will be many who will.

Accept Your Uniqueness

Accepting your uniqueness means loving yourself for who you are unconditionally. It doesn't matter if you're not where you want to be right now, we're all a work in progress. Accept all your weaknesses, even though you're still working on them. Accept your appearance, from your face to your feet. Embrace your quirks, likes, dislikes, and fantasies. Only once you accept yourself, can you expect others to accept you.

Seek Out Your Tribe

No matter how unusual, weird, or random your interests are, you're probably not the only one on this planet who has them. The internet is at your disposal, use it to connect with some like-minded people. You can search the internet for content and communities related to your interests. If you don't find anything, create a YouTube channel for like-minded people. Start a website or set up a vibrant Instagram account. Post about your hobbies on Threads. Eventually, the people you want to connect with will seek you out.

Learn to Deal With Criticism Well

When you dare to walk your own path waving your freak flag, there are bound to be some people who will disapprove. There will always be people ready to pass judgment on those who choose not to be like them. These nay-saying, negativity-spreading individuals may hate on you because they feel resentful towards you for having the courage to be yourself. Accept and acknowledge that everyone has a right to an opinion, and keep walking your path. Eventually, when everyone sees that you are self-assured, confident and not seeking approval from anyone, they will leave you alone. Perhaps you may even inspire others to embrace their uniqueness too.

CULTIVATING SELF-COMPASSION

Self-compassion involves treating yourself with kindness, and acknowledging that, like everyone else, you make mistakes and face difficulties. It means being mindful of your own thoughts and emotions and allowing yourself to process them with patience and understanding.

The Importance of Self-Compassion

It Helps Build Emotional Strength

About 20% of teens in the US are victims of bullying (StopBullying, 2019). While you can't control the actions of other people, you can control how you respond to them. There is a considerable chance that you are experiencing, have experienced, or will at some point experience bullying. How ready are you to cope with the potential effects of these interactions on your mental, emotional, and physical health?

Will you absorb every hurtful word, like a sponge or will you let them slide, like water off a duck's back? Having self-compassion helps you to look at bullying from a critical point of view. Only from a place of self-compassion can you see that bullies, by their hurtful words, are actually masking their own insecurities and flaws while expressing the pain and anger they have inside.

It Improves Your Self-Image

Being self-compassionate means forgiving yourself for your shortcomings, big and small. It means seeing yourself as a human being, worthy of second chances, love, and acceptance. Self-compassion stops you from being too judgmental toward yourself and helps you to see yourself in a more positive light.

Promotes Healthy Coping Mechanisms

Challenges and difficulties are inevitable in all of our lives. The term coping mechanism refers to how individuals manage and adapt to difficult situations. While we all face difficulties at some point, we tend to use different coping mechanisms. Some people develop unhealthy coping mechanisms such as alcoholism and drugs to 'escape' from their situation. But when you have self-compassion, you will never go for dangerous, unhealthy, or self-harming means to cope with your problems. Instead during times like this, you will find healthy ways to cope that help you maintain your well-being.

Lower Your Stress Levels

Being compassionate toward yourself means not expecting yourself to be perfect. You are human and entitled to have learning curves, make mistakes, and take a break. You gaze upon your feelings with kindness and understanding. So, naturally, you'll know you're doing the best you can and avoid unnecessary stress.

PRACTICAL TOOL: AFFIRMATIONS

Affirmations are positive statements that can help you challenge and overcome negative thoughts. When you repeat these statements daily, they end up becoming engraved in your subconscious mind. Over time, the repetition disrupts the cycle of negative thinking, replacing it with a positive one, and inspiring you to take action.

Repeating phrases such as "I am worthy of love and respect" every night may sound incredibly silly. However, it is scientifically proven to be an effective way to help lower your stress levels and boost your academic performance (Moore, 2019). In other words, if people use affirmations to treat depression, low self-esteem, and other mental health problems, it won't hurt to give it a try.

Examples of when to use affirmations:

- When you want to boost your self-confidence and self-esteem
- When you want to be more productive at school
- When you're building healthier habits
- When you're trying to overcome anxiety

15 Self-Compassion Affirmations

Boost your mental well-being with these affirmations, crafted to help you navigate challenges, build inner strength, and foster a healthier relationship with yourself.

1. I am doing the best that I can.
2. I embrace the best and worst parts of myself.
3. I accept my past and I am excited about my future.
4. I am grateful to be me.
5. I have nothing to prove.
6. I am kind to myself just as I am kind to others.
7. I give myself permission to grow and develop.

8. I honor myself by making time throughout my day to rest.
9. I am strong and resilient.
10. I am my own best friend and number one fan.
11. I practice self-compassion by nourishing my body with healthy and delicious foods.
12. I radiate confidence and self-assurance.
13. I am a loving person, and that love starts with myself.
14. It is okay for me to feel my feelings.
15. I am attractive, just as I am.

Tips to Write Your Own Affirmations and Use Affirmations

These affirmations may not be exactly what you need and, in that case, you can always write your own affirmations. Don't worry, it's super easy and won't take a lot of time. All you have to do is follow the tips below:

1. Base your affirmations on aspects of your life that you'd like to change.
2. Affirmations work within the parameters of what is possible. So ensure your affirmations are statements that you believe.
3. Write using positive language. Instead of "I will not be afraid" rather write "I will be courageous."
4. Write in the present tense.
5. Include feelings in your affirmations. Use emotive words.
6. Repeat your affirmations at least once a day. You may choose to recite them from memory, read them, or

write them down. You can choose to display them on your bathroom mirror, write them on cards to fit in your wallet, or access them through a mobile app.

IN SUMMARY

In this chapter, we've explored what it means to embrace uniqueness. Navigating through the benefits and challenges that social media presents in your life and discussing ways to deal with challenges with a dose of self-compassion are all valuable tools for your journey. Finally, you learned how to use affirmations as a strategy to train yourself to think positively. In the upcoming chapter, we'll delve into the art of cultivating unwavering self-confidence.

3

SLAY BAE! UNLEASHING YOUR INNER CONFIDENCE

> *Imperfection is beauty, madness is genius and it's better to be absolutely ridiculous than absolutely boring.*
>
> — MARILYN MONROE

THE CONFIDENCE CONUNDRUM

Yolanda, a 13-year-old, shares how her confidence eroded after she began comparing herself to the other girls in her class.

Lately, I've been feeling a heavy sense of self-doubt. It's like a shadow that clings to me no matter what I do. I remember being very confident, but now, I'm left mentally worn out by how often I wonder if I'm good enough. It seems the mirror only reflects my insecurities, and I feel so hopeless because I don't think I measure up to other 13-year-old girls.

I try to hide my sadness, anxiety, and disappointment from my parents because I don't want them to worry. Even though they can't see how I feel inside, they've sensed a change in me. Whenever they ask if I'm okay, I say "I'm fine" with a forced smile.

One evening after dinner, my mom asked me how I was doing. I initially brushed her off, but she persisted. She said that I didn't look as happy and excited about going to school as I used to.

At that moment, I couldn't hold back any longer. Tears welled up, and I poured out my feelings to her. My mom listened with unwavering support, assuring me it was okay to feel this way. She shared that everyone struggles with self-esteem at some point, emphasizing there was no shame in it.

Her support and understanding made me feel at peace. She said she loved me just the way I was. She also suggested we visit a therapist together, so I could help navigate my negative feelings and work on rebuilding my self-esteem.

Talking to someone turned out to be just what I needed. My therapy sessions have guided me in changing my inner dialogue and focusing on my strengths rather than obsessing over my flaws.

My self-confidence and self-esteem still have plenty of room for improvement, but I'm feeling so much better. I'm grateful that my mom stood by me when I needed her most, helping me find my way back to self-confidence.

WHAT IS CONFIDENCE?

Confidence is the belief that you will succeed or that you have made the correct decision in a specific situation. Throughout a person's life, their confidence levels may change, going from overconfidence to low confidence and back again. The life experiences we encounter and our reactions to them can greatly influence our confidence levels.

Picture a complex gear system, with individual gears representing self-esteem, resilience, self-compassion, and confidence. They are interconnected so that when one gear turns, it triggers a ripple effect. When self-compassion rotates, it nudges resilience, which, in turn, sets confidence into motion. This illustration shows the interdependence that exists between confidence and self-esteem, self-compassion, and resilience.

A Vivid Example of How Confidence, Self-Esteem, Self-Compassion, and Resilience Are Interlinked

Imagine it's the last exam of the semester and the room is buzzing with excitement for the upcoming school break, and as you take your seat, just minutes before the exam, you feel the tension build. The AC is a bit too strong, and you feel goosebumps on your arms. Minutes later, your teacher arrives. You sit up straighter in your seat. As part of the mandatory procedure, your teacher starts droning, "Alright, please check that you don't have any unauthorized material..." The next thing you know, a thick question paper is slapped onto your table and just looking at it you break a cold sweat.

You suddenly doubt whether you're prepared enough. You think back with regret to the long study break you took to watch a movie the previous night. But, recognizing your self-doubt, you take a deep calming breath. You tell yourself that you did do your best and it's okay to feel nervous before an exam—exercising self-compassion. As you remember all your previous accomplishments, you begin to feel convinced that you have it in you to make it through the exam. The little voice in your head says "I can do this. I totally have this under control." —relying on your self-esteem.

"It is now 9 a.m., you may start," booms the teacher, disrupting your mental pep talk. Your heart doesn't even skip a beat, you're ready for this. As you progress through the exam, the questions get more difficult. You get to a question that you don't know how to answer, but instead of giving up and losing hope, you choose not to waste more time on it and move on to answer others—showing resilience.

You think clearly and feel a sense of calmness during the exam. You're not shaky because thanks to your self-esteem, resilience, and self-compassion you feel assured that you're able to pass the exam—exhibiting confidence.

Five Characteristics of Self-Confidence In Teens

Confident Teens Are Not Followers

Confidence enables a teen to firmly stand by their values and beliefs when they are faced with opposing views or peer pressure. Confident teens have the courage to stand by what they think is right, even and especially when they have to stand alone.

Imagine this: You're strolling through your neighborhood with your friends, and you notice a group of kids playing pranks on a blind man who's walking alone. The kids set up obstacles in his path, and whenever the man's cane encounters these, the kids burst into laughter as he changes direction. Your friends find it hilarious and rush to take out their phones to record what's happening.

You feel your anger rising quickly. Do you pretend to laugh with your friends because you don't have the guts to stand up to them and those kids? Or do you reproach your friends, storm over, and explain to the blind man what was happening while you help him get home?

Confident Teens Have Leadership Potential

Teens who are self-assured are more likely to be comfortable leading others in roles such as class representative, or any other leadership position they may have access to.

Furthermore, other teenagers are more likely to respect the authority of confident teens, meaning that teens who are confident often find themselves nominated by their peers for leadership roles—sometimes even without them having shown any interest. People naturally seek confidence in leaders as it inspires positivity, safety, and progress.

Confident Teens Are More Motivated and Ambitious

With a heightened belief in their abilities, confident teens are more likely to set ambitious goals for their future. These teens aspire to achieve more in various areas of their lives, such as academics, sports, and personal projects. Confidence makes teens more willing to work persistently on their goals, making them more likely to achieve what they put their minds to.

Take Jessy as an example. In his junior year of high school, Jessy was slightly overweight. His goal was to make the soccer team in his senior year. Jessy had played soccer back in the early days of elementary school but had gained weight after puberty. He didn't look in the slightest athletic, and everyone he told about his goal was skeptical. But Jessy's confidence in himself pushed him to work hard because he believed he could achieve his goal. To achieve your goals, you must have a belief in yourself that is much stronger than those around you!

Confident Teens Bounce Back From Setbacks and Disappointments Faster

Confident teens tend to handle setbacks and failures better, as they view setbacks as opportunities for growth rather than insurmountable obstacles. The positive attitude that inevitably comes from confidence will contribute to your mental and emotional well-being and ultimately help you build resilience.

Confident Teens Are More Independent and Self-Reliant

Confident teenagers are more willing to take initiative, solve problems on their own, and navigate the transition into adulthood with greater self-assurance. After graduating high school, teens are expected to attend college or start working. Once you start corresponding with potential employers and colleges, you will need to be able to communicate effectively, express self-assuredness, and articulate your qualifications. In general, confident teens will be more successful in accomplishing important milestones on their own and becoming independent, than teens who lack self-confidence.

The Struggles Teens Face In Building Confidence

Absence of Parental Care and Support

The home is the first place a child begins to develop their identity and self-esteem. Younger children are fully dependent on their caregivers to guide them in developing a sense of identity. Through interactions with their mothers, fathers, or primary caregivers, children learn important things about themselves.

Teens who belong to families in which they are consistently reprimanded, reminded of their weaknesses, or told what they can and cannot do, are more likely to have low self-esteem and low confidence. On the other hand, teens who develop in supportive families where they are praised for the good they do, consistently reminded of their strengths, and encouraged to explore their interests are more likely to have higher self-esteem and self-confidence.

Although it's possible to gain confidence at any time in life, the early formative years of a child's life are important in helping them develop their confidence.

Self-Image

Social media is largely responsible for providing the perfect image of the "ideal" appearance that teens compare themselves to. These "ideal" beauty standards are unrealistic and unhealthy. Teens are often not aware of the unhealthy behaviors, health risks, and mental health issues that people who have attained those idealized looks go through. So, when a teen with a negative self-image compares themselves to these ideals, it's likely to impact their self-confidence.

Take Gladys, for instance, a sixteen-year-old girl who wants to audition for the lead role in her school play. She's played powerful supporting roles in her acting club's annual show, for which she received plenty of praise. She knows she's talented, but Gladys doesn't think she's pretty enough to be the lead. She's afraid to audition because she believes she'll lose the role to someone who is seen as prettier, even if they aren't half as talented as she is. Her fear gets the best of her, and she never auditions. Years later, reminiscing as an adult, she wishes she had taken her shot, who knows what would have happened?

Discrimination

Being mistreated for things like your race, gender, sexuality, religion or beliefs is not only unfair but can negatively impact anyone's self-confidence. Discrimination screams "You are not accepted, beautiful, worthy, relevant, wanted, tolerated, loved, respected, or significant because of who you are." It's a violation of human rights, for many reasons, and it is something you should never tolerate.

The Confidence-Crushing Myths

There are plenty of false beliefs that people have about confidence, below we debunk some of the myths that may be holding you back from embracing self-confidence.

Self-Confidence Is Inherent

Some of your characteristics are determined by genetics and can never be altered, such as your height or your eye color—unless you go for color lenses, of course. Your level of confidence, however, is not one of those characteristics. Research has proven that genetics can only contribute up to 50% of a person's level of confidence (May, 2023). Meaning that your genes can only be 50% responsible for your current level of confidence. The remaining percentage is determined by you. Our level of confidence is not set in stone. Nobody is destined to lack confidence, and you should never accept it as part of "who you are."

You First Have to Achieve Great Success to Be Confident

Just like it's possible to have achieved epic success and still lack confidence, it's similarly possible to feel confident after small wins. This is because the immediate gratification from short-term goals eventually builds your confidence and provides you with the drive and focus to conquer larger objectives. Moreover, this specific myth can plunge you into a stagnant cycle. How? It's like this, you're waiting to achieve big things to gain confidence, but it takes confidence to achieve big things. Get it?

Once You Get Your Confidence to 'High' It Stays There

Humans change continuously and adapt to life events. Similarly, your confidence fluctuates in different situations. Believe it or not, even a highly confident person experiences moments in which they feel intense self-doubt. People who lack resilience give up on their endeavors when their confidence reaches a low point but building your level of resilience will reduce skepticism, self-doubt, and negativity.

Being Confident Means Being Loud and Aggressive

Confidence requires assertiveness. If you're assertive, you know how to express your point of view clearly and directly, while still respecting others. You can have a high level of quiet confidence without overstepping boundaries, hurting others feelings, or demanding the attention of the room.

BUT THE VOICES IN MY HEAD...ALL ABOUT POSITIVE SELF-TALK

Self-talk is your inner voice; the conversations you have with yourself. Although self-talk is a continuous internal dialogue, you have the power to control the words you use when you talk to yourself because they influence your emotions, beliefs, decisions, and actions. Your inner thoughts can be positive, like when you encourage yourself to solve a problem, or they can be negative, like when you doubt yourself or worry.

Oftentimes we are not aware of our inner dialogue, because we don't consider ourselves independent and separate from these voices. So when our critical inner voice tells us "You're not going to make it, so why would you even bother," you think it must be true.

The truth is that the negative thoughts in our heads don't represent our true selves. Instead, they are manifestations of low self-esteem, poor body image, low self-compassion, a lack of resilience, internalized insecurities, and negative emotions such as fear. Identifying these negative voices as separate from yourself will help you single out individual thoughts and reframe them into positive ones.

Importance of Positive Self-Talk for Confidence

Positive self-talk boosts self-confidence by encouraging an optimistic mindset. This means using affirmations like, "I can handle this presentation; I've prepared thoroughly."

It helps counter self-doubt and anxiety, empowering you to tackle challenges. So you can tell yourself, "I may not have all the answers, but I'm capable of learning and figuring things out."

By reinforcing self-belief, positive self-talk enhances resilience and promotes a can-do attitude. So you can't help but know, "I've faced challenges before and overcome them; I can handle whatever comes my way."

How to Reframe Negative Thoughts Into Positive Ones

Below are some questions that can help you escape the distorted reality your negative thinking wants you to believe, and refocus on the positive side of things.

Test how realistic your thoughts are:

- Is there credible evidence to support this idea?
- If you were to objectively evaluate your thoughts, could you discredit them?
- Why should I trust my negative predictions of the future?

See the bigger picture:

- What's the worst thing that could happen?
- What's the best thing that could happen?
- What's most likely to happen, based on the information I have?
- Is there anything good about this situation?
- Will this matter in five years?

CONFIDENCE-BOOSTING STRATEGIES

Practice Safe Comparisons

Comparing yourself to others is something we all do and can be a valuable tool for self-reflection and personal growth. Comparisons may inspire us to cultivate qualities we admire in others. However, when comparisons lead to feelings of inadequacy and self-doubt, it's time to stop.

Take Safe Risks

Get out of your comfort zone and try something you've never tried before. Put yourself in situations where your voice will be heard like engaging in class discussions. Take on a leadership role or commit to a new responsibility like serving as a treasurer for a student association or joining the student government. Randomly strike up conversations with different people from your class or even with upperclassmen——it's only as awkward as you make it.

Dare to Be Authentic

In nature, animals such as zebras and buffalos blend in with their herd as a way to survive. A zebra born without stripes can easily be singled out from the herd and become an automatic target for predators. As humans, we are not reliant on blending in as a survival strategy. Thanks to the uniqueness of our thoughts, ideas, and dreams, we have amazing art, technology, and improvements in countless areas of human life. So be proud and unapologetically you.

Shake Off Self-Doubt

Self-doubt comes from believing that you're likely to fail. Often, you'll find that this belief of definite failure doesn't even need evidence to stick. For example, you're thinking of trying public speaking for the first time, but you have thoughts like "You'll probably forget your words and make a fool of yourself." Ask yourself, how can you be so sure you'll fail if you've never tried it before? Think of all the things you tried and succeeded at to give you perspective.

PARENTS/TEACHERS: HOW TO HELP YOUR TEEN DEVELOP SELF-CONSCIOUSNESS

Love Unconditionally

Your teen will have greater confidence in uncovering their identity, learning new things, and getting out of their comfort zone if you let them know that you'll love them no matter what they decide to do, who they decide to be, and wherever they aspire to go. Think of your unconditional love as a safety net beneath them as they climb to higher levels of self-awareness and independence.

Encourage Them to Gain New Skills and Sharpen Their Existing Ones

Your teen may have skills that they can use as a means of income in the future. Encourage them to strengthen those skill sets and celebrate them for good effort. If your teen doesn't know their way around basic things like budgeting, changing a lightbulb, calling a tow-truck, or any other seemingly insignificant but important skill, teach them. The more they feel they can handle, control, and understand their lives, the more independent they'll feel.

Show That It's Unacceptable to Quit

When your teen complains that something is hard, encourage them to accomplish it. Don't run to their rescue and find a way to take them out of every demanding situation. Letting them handle it shows them that you have confidence in their abilities.

Give Less Advice

It's tempting to point out all the pitfalls in your teen's path because you've already been through it and you want to make things easier for them. But by doing this you risk being the helicopter parent, always hovering over their children. Teens need to practice making their own decisions and experiencing the outcomes.

PRACTICAL TOOL: CONFIDENCE-BUILDING EXERCISES

There are many ways you can help your teen build their self-confidence. Below is a guide to help you facilitate their growth, it includes activities boosting both social connection and introspection.

Certificate of Recognition

Assign each student a secret partner to observe for a week. They should each take note of anything good their partners do. On Friday, the students give and receive their certificates. The following week the students perform the same exercise but observe themselves instead. This exercise helps train the brain to seek out the positive aspects and acknowledge even minor achievements and successes.

Gratitude Journal

There's a positive relationship between gratitude and self-esteem. Encouraging teens to note three things they're grateful for can significantly boost their happiness and satisfaction with life. Prompts such as "Something that made me smile today was..."

Letter to Yourself

This exercise fosters self-acceptance which is pivotal in developing self-confidence. Have teens write three letters addressed to themselves. Address one to their past selves, teens should reflect on events they are proud of, ashamed of, and what they learned. The letter to their present self aims at acknowledging the good in them and celebrating how far they've come. In the last letter, teens address their future selves detailing what they want to achieve at the end of the school year.

Board Games

Playing board games in a group strengthens a teen's social skills. It provides opportunities for individuals to talk, who perhaps would never have in normal circumstances. Teens are likely to feel more confident when they feel comfortable in social interactions.

Random Act of Kindness

Being of service to others and showing kindness is a great way to boost a teen's confidence. Encourage teens to keep their random acts of kindness to themselves, to ensure their motivations are free of vanity.

IN SUMMARY

In this chapter, we delved into the multifaceted world of confidence, exploring its definition, the hurdles that often obstruct your path toward it, and the myths that may cloud your understanding. Uncovering the transformative power of positive self-talk and how it can nurture the seeds of self-assuredness within you is an essential part of the confidence revolution. Armed with the strategies we've discussed, you're equipped to take each step with newfound determination and resilience. The next chapter covers stress, exploring how we can use our newfound confidence to control it.

4

NOT TODAY, BRUH! TAMING THE STRESS MONSTER

> *Worrying about outcomes over which I have no control is punishing myself before the universe has decided I ought to be punished.*
>
> — SHERRY THOMAS

DEALING WITH ACADEMIC PRESSURE

Poppy, a high school senior, shares how the stress from the pressure to succeed helped her prioritize her mental health.

School used to be fun, a place where I could just be myself, hang out with friends, and crack jokes. I'm all about that extrovert life, feeding off conversations, laughter, and goofing around. But that all changed in my sophomore year.

I switched to this super intense charter school, hoping for a place where I could really learn and thrive. Little did I know, it was all about grades, tests, and impressing college admission boards. It was like a constant race, everyone comparing SAT scores, AP classes, and who did the most volunteering.

My junior year? That's when I went all in, thinking I had to focus on school even more, get those top grades, and get ready for college. I mean, it wasn't healthy, but it felt like the only way to survive. The pressure was everywhere, from the constant discussions about college prep to the never-ending competition.

I watched friends stressing over a B, and staying up all night, and it scared me. Soon, "old Poppy" was fading away. I withdrew from friends, got anxious in the lunchroom, and had these moments where I'd overthink everything and end up in tears.

Senior year was crazy, you know? Everyone was gunning for those perfect A's, dreaming of Ivy League colleges like it was the only way to go. I felt the heat, big time! It was like 24/7, eat, sleep, and breathe academics.

I knew something had to change. I wanted the "old Poppy" back, the one who cracked jokes and sang songs. I couldn't let this stress define me. So, I started speaking up, fighting for more mental health support in school.

I realized that this toxic academic pressure wasn't the only way. It shouldn't cost our well-being, and it shouldn't make students suffer in silence. It was time for a change, and I was ready to be part of it.

UNDERSTANDING STRESS

Stress is how your mind and body react when you feel overwhelmed or under pressure. It can arise whenever you doubt your ability to fulfill your responsibilities or start worrying about what will happen if you fail. Basically, stress happens when the demands placed on you are more than you can comfortably handle. These demands can either be self-imposed or imposed upon you by your family, school, or society.

Stress, on its own, is not a bad thing. However, experiencing it over a long period of time can have negative mental and physical effects. Stress is considered long-term (chronic) if you experience it for a number of hours a day, consistently for weeks, or months. Short-term (acute) stress is what you experience between a few minutes and a few hours.

In stressful situations that are high-risk or threatening, your brain secretes a stress hormone called adrenaline. Adrenaline helps to ensure your survival by making your heart beat faster, increasing the energy and oxygen supply to your brain and muscles. The temporary effects are increased strength, immunity to pain, and hyper-alertness.

However, prolonged exposure to stress hormones and the resulting long-term activation of your body's stress responses can disrupt almost every bodily function. Likely making any existing medical condition worse. Skin conditions such as acne and eczema may flare up, people who have epilepsy may experience more seizures and mental health conditions such as depression may be triggered. Under stress, your body kind of malfunctions. The longer you experience this intense stress, the more health problems are likely to emerge.

The Difference Between Teen and Adult Stress

Teenage brains release more of the stress hormone cortisol during times of stress than adult brains (ReachOut, n.d.). High levels of cortisol cause weight gain, acne, irritability, and difficulty concentrating. What's more, researchers who tested the impact of cortisol levels on decision-making found that higher levels of cortisol reduce our capacity to make decisions (Putman et al., 2009). This means that teens can potentially struggle more with critical and clear thinking when they're stressed than adults.

When teens experience stress they're more likely to develop unhealthy coping mechanisms such as alcohol and drug abuse. Behaviors such as these can also lead to addiction, which may make mental health issues such as anxiety and depression worse.

Teen stress is something that's often overlooked since the symptoms are very much the same as the normal hormone fluctuations that teens experience. So while it may be easier for an adult to recognize when they are stressed, teens may experience stress symptoms and not know that stress is the cause of these feelings.

What Causes Stress In Teens?

Academics (Grades, Tests, Homework)

Teens often get stressed out by the pressure to get good grades in school. Instead of enjoying the learning experience, they worry about fulfilling the high expectations that their family or they themselves have set. This can feel overwhelming, and ironically, the added stress actually makes it harder for teens to perform well in academics.

Social Relationships

Adolescence is when teens discover who they are and how they fit in with their peers and society. Some teens may find it hard to find their place in the social environment at their school. In a place where everyone has a group, teens who are struggling to make and keep friends may experience extreme anxiety and stress when trying to socialize. Additionally, teens who have begun exploring romantic and/or sexual relationships can add a layer of major sources of stress.

Negative Feelings and Thoughts About Themselves

During adolescence, a teen's self-esteem tends to fluctuate. Low self-esteem is usually experienced together with the pressure to conform to beauty standards or try to fit in with 'cool' kids. Teen boys who try to suppress their authentic selves, in an effort to be accepted in a group are more likely to experience stress. The same is true for teen girls trying to look like the idealized standard of beauty. Similarly, LGBTQ teens navigating societal expectations and struggling to express their true identities may also face challenges to their self-esteem. The pressure to conform to heteronormative norms can contribute to feelings of isolation and stress within this community, emphasizing the importance of fostering inclusive and accepting environments for all adolescents.

Life's Challenges

Sometimes, life's lemons can't easily be made into lemonade. Family events like parents divorcing, moving schools, illness, death of a loved one, and financial problems can become sources of immense stress to teens. Often, these life-changing events are beyond anyone's control, and teens may become stressed as they grapple with the aftermath.

Lack of Sleep

Sleeping is like paying a debt. Every night you are owed at least eight hours of sleep. Sleeping for fewer hours leaves you with an outstanding sleep debt. Over time, as you continue to deprive your body of sleep, the effects of insufficient sleep may begin to catch up on you. Sleep deprivation can also worsen existing mental health disorders such as depression, anxiety, and paranoia.

Recognizing the Signs of Teen Stress

The first step in dealing with stress is recognizing the signs in your own body and behavior—this is the same for teens as it is for adults. While each teen deals with stress differently, parents and teens should be able to notice a change. Read the following and take note of when you might have experienced these signs of stress.

- Disengaged: Are you feeling emotionally detached? Do you suddenly feel like you don't care about anything anymore? Do you feel like a dull version of your former self?
- Change in appetite: Stress can lead to either a loss of appetite or a big increase in appetite. One end of the extreme may lead to unhealthy weight loss, while the other end may lead to obesity. Have you noticed any changes in your meals, portion size, and how much you snack?
- Withdrawn: Stress can drain you, leaving you with little energy for socializing. Do you interact with others as much as you used to? Do you feel like you're avoiding people and spending more time in your room and on your phones?
- Spending less time on hobbies: Stressed teens tend to dwell on their stressors, and everything else including the things they enjoyed before, fade away and seem irrelevant. Have a look at your regular weekly routine. Do you go out or have friends over as often as you did before? Do you still help out at home like you used to? Do you play games or spend time with your younger siblings?
- Insomnia: Stress is a major cause of insomnia, in both teens and adults. When you experience insomnia for long periods of time, you're more likely to develop anxiety-related mental health disorders. If you're

unsure if your sleeping habits have changed, try keeping a sleep diary where you keep track of what time you fell asleep and woke up, how many hours you've slept, and your quality of sleep.
- Depression: Stress disrupts your healthy coping mechanisms. For example, increased academic stress could make you stop doing mood-boosting activities such as exercising, hanging out with friends, baking, playing with pets, etc. In the absence of activities that improve your mood, you could slip into depression.
- For Parents/ Teachers: Common signs of depression to look out for include difficulty maintaining focus and remembering things, avoiding social events they used to enjoy, lethargy, and self-harming behaviors.

Stress in the Teenage Jungle

Prepare to enter a typical day in the life of a teenager. How well do you relate to any of these feelings and experiences?

School Stressors

Justin, 17

With a clumsy hand, you turn off your alarm clock. It's Monday morning already but you hardly slept a wink. In a frenzy, you take a shower, brush your teeth, go downstairs for breakfast, and bolt out the door. You're on your way to school, but unlike when you were little, you're dreading going to school.

As you sit in the first class of the day, you try to listen to your teacher introduce a new topic in chemistry class. You're filled with dread because you still haven't mastered the last three topics, and now here's a new one. You glance at the exam date written in the top right-hand corner of the whiteboard. Your stomach clenches violently. You're trying to calm down, but deep down you're panicking. Will you be able to pass this class?

You soldier through the day. In the restroom, you change into your volleyball uniform and head out to the pitch. Practice goes well, but looking at your watch dampens your mood. You still have community service at the animal shelter, and that new chemistry topic is still lurching in the shadows of your mind. Restlessly, a wave of anxiety comes over you and you wonder, "Will I make it home in time to study?"

Social Stressors

Jessica, 15

As you turn a corner and walk down the hallway, you spot your friends at the other end of the hallway, cracking up just outside your locker. You're glad to see them and walk a little faster toward them. When you get a little closer, they spot you and smile. But wait, they don't look like they were expecting to see you. A girl from a different class walks over to them and they all walk away together. You're slapped by the cold realization that it wasn't you they were waiting for.

Eric, 17

Your phone buzzes and your heart skips a beat, you hope it's your girlfriend but it's your mom. You wonder why your girlfriend hasn't been texting you back. You think about how your friend said that they saw her at a coffee shop with one of your teammates. Could she be seeing someone else? Is that why she's ignoring you? Your stomach flips as you realize you could be losing her. What did you do wrong?

Abby, 16

If you had set a timer when you began staring into the mirror, it would now read fifteen minutes. You're getting late for school but you can't stop wishing away the new pimple that erupted right next to your nose. You consider spending the day at home and lying about having a stomachache. But today's the submission date for your assignment. You have to go or risk getting hell from your history teacher. You try to cover it up with makeup, but you know it's no use. Just the thought of walking into class with that red bump on your face makes you break out in sweat.

Home Stressors

Norah, 15

As you head home, you hope today's the day your parents sign a peace treaty. The arguing, name-calling, tears, and smashed plates, cups, or lamps are becoming a daily routine at your house and you feel caught in the middle. You once dreaded the prospect of your parents getting a divorce, but now you think maybe it's the best for everyone. You wonder what a divorce would mean for you and your siblings. Will you have to move? Will you see both of your parents as often? All these questions swirl around in your head until you release a deep sigh, and realize you've been holding your breath.

Stress is the uninvited guest that often shows up when we're trying to stretch our limited time and energy to cover a lengthy to-do list. The weight of knowing that today's performance can significantly shape our future adds to the pressure we feel. Beyond that, there are parts of life we wish to change but can't control, such as our physical appearance and home situation. These desires can become additional sources of stress.

But it doesn't end there. Our emotional well-being is directly linked to our relationships with others, whether it's with romantic partners or friends. The dynamics within these connections can also have an impact, and conflicts or misunderstandings in these areas can undoubtedly elevate our stress levels.

PARENTS/TEACHERS: HOW TO RECOGNIZE DEPRESSION

While any teen can develop depression, some teens are more at risk due to a number of factors that can make them more susceptible. Make sure to be especially vigilant if two or more of the risk factors below apply to your teen.

- Depression or other mood disorders run in your family.
- Your teen has recently experienced a stressful life event like the death of a loved one, separating parents, bullying, a breakup, or failing classes in school.
- They have low self-esteem and self-image.
- You have a teenage daughter; teen girls are twice as likely as boys to have depression.

- Your teen is anti-social.
- They have learning difficulties or a chronic illness.
- Any other form of tension in the family.

Signs of Depression in Teens

Depressed teens commonly display the following symptoms. Take some time to observe them, and if you notice these symptoms persisting for longer than two weeks, seek professional help from a doctor.

- Increased sensitivity to criticism.
- Withdrawing from the people closest to them like their parents and friends.
- Feeling tired or lethargic most of the time.
- Sudden bursts of anger, and a constant buzz of irritability.
- Loss of joy from their favorite activities or hobbies.
- Feeling sad for most of the day.
- Change in appetite, eating too much or too little.
- Drop in school grades, and neglecting schoolwork.
- Engaging in high-risk behaviors such as staying out late drinking, experimenting with drugs, and recklessness.
- Change in sleeping pattern, insomnia, or excessive sleeping.

How To Recognize Anxiety Disorder

According to information from the National Institutes of Health (NIH), almost one-third of adolescents between the ages of 13 and 18 are likely to have an anxiety disorder. While anxiety is fairly common in teens, it's important to monitor your teen to ensure it doesn't progress to a point where it disrupts their ability to focus in school, hinders their social interactions with friends, and takes away from the enjoyment of life.

Signs of Anxiety in Teens

The primary sign is persistent worrying or tension for a minimum of six months, even with little or no apparent reason. Teens suffering from anxiety often find that while their anxiety remains, the issues they worry about change, whether it's school, finances, family, relationships, or physical appearance. When the issue perceived to be causing the anxiety gets resolved, another often takes its place.

Other signs include:

- Problems concentrating in school or elsewhere
- Fatigue (caused by a prolonged state of mental and body tension)
- Irritability
- Insomnia or restless and unsatisfying sleep
- Restlessness when awake

While this guideline offers a good reference to help you keep an eye out for your teen's mental health, it's not exhaustive. Know that as a parent or teacher, you have a deep understanding of your teenager, making you well-equipped to identify any additional unusual behaviors that may not be listed here.

HOW YOU CAN BEAT STRESS AS A TEEN

Take Deep Breaths

This may sound too simple to work, but deep breathing is an effective way to slow down your heart rate and relax your muscles. Follow the easy steps below to practice deep breathing for near-instant stress relief.

1. Find a comfy spot. Sit with your feet on the floor, close your eyes, and let your hands rest on your thighs.
2. Take a slow breath in through your nose. Feel your chest and belly expand as your lungs fill. You can count to five or whatever feels right.
3. Now, breathe out slowly, either through your nose or mouth, whichever feels better. Count during the exhale and make it at least as long as you inhale.
4. If your mind drifts away. Just bring your thoughts back to your breath.
5. Keep doing this for a few minutes.
6. Afterward, check in with yourself. Does your brain and body feel more relaxed?

Exercise

Exercise triggers your brain's release of feel-good hormones called endorphins. Apart from feeling good, exercise helps you burn out your stress hormones, leaving you feeling energetic, and less burdened by worries. So whenever you feel stressed about an upcoming test, but too panicked to actually study, exercise. Exercise every morning before school to help you focus better. Exercise even when you feel pressed for time.

Get a Good Night's Sleep

Insufficient sleep can make you irritable and make your brain feel foggy. You need sleep to replenish the energy you use up during the day. Here are some tips to help you sleep better:

- Have a hot shower about an hour before bed to relax your muscles and help you fall asleep.
- Use your bed only for sleeping to train your brain to start quieting down as soon as you get under the covers. This means avoiding doing homework, thinking about social media, or anything that's not sleeping on your bed.

Be More Optimistic

Stress comes from worrying about the worst things that could happen, such as failing a class, not getting into your dream college, or never finding true love, among others. When you have no way to know what's going to happen in your future, why not choose to believe in positive outcomes?

Write About It

There's magic in putting pen to paper, it's like you're physically channeling your overflowing emotions onto a page. Expressing yourself through writing can even help reduce stress and boost your overall well-being. A stressful time is a great time to start journaling if you aren't already. If you have a journal, consider making daily entries in which you talk about your day and how you feel.

Talk About It

Dealing with overwhelming pressure is tough, and it's important not to add to your burden by keeping your feelings inside. When you lock your emotions away, they can build up until they reach a breaking point. This can lead to mental health issues like anxiety, depression, and self-destructive behaviors. That is why it's important to find as many ways as possible to express what you feel inside and expel those negative emotions that are causing stress. Talk to a trusted friend, a teacher, your parents, or anyone who you can trust.

Set Time Aside For Leisure

You need time for fun! Give your brain and body a break once in a while and do something you enjoy. Life is too short to waste on feeling stressed, unwell, and unhappy. Achieving great things doesn't always have to be linked to stress, and having a healthy schedule with ample time to relax does not mean that you're a slacker. In fact, when you practice stress-relief methods, you actually energize your brain and clear it from the fog that stress hormones cause, boosting your memory retention and concentration.

Get a Support System

Every tree that stands tall and firm is supported by a large network of roots just below the surface. Humans are not meant to be islands, we're social creatures who need love, acceptance, and support from others. Don't forget to take care of your relationships with your friends and family. When you're there for them when they need a shoulder to lean on, they will do the same for you when you need it most. You can also join a support group for young people who are also experiencing extreme stress. Having a sense of community will help you feel less isolated, and like "We're all in this together."

Find Creative Outlets

Creative activities like painting, drawing, or playing music provide an outlet where you can express complex emotions that you may find too challenging to articulate verbally. Engaging in the creativity process fosters mindfulness, momentarily diverting your attention from life's stressors. The emotional release and sense of accomplishment you get from sharing your art—whether it's painting, a song, pottery, or any other form—makes it so worth it.

PARENTS/TEACHERS: HOW TO HELP YOUR TEEN OVERCOME STRESS

As a parent, you can't physically take away your teen's stress but there are ways that you can help and support them.

- Model healthy coping mechanisms: Be an example to them of how to use healthy coping mechanisms and stress management tools. Let your teen see what you do to maintain your mental health and well-being.
- Be a lighthouse parent: Like before, we encourage you to follow the lighthouse parenting style. Allow your teen to make decisions and solve their own problems, because it's the only way they'll be able to gain confidence. With a strong sense of confidence, your teen will be better equipped to deal with their life's stressors, with or without you.
- Give them a media education: The media is a large part of your teen's life; however, they often misinterpret what they see and hear. As a parent or teacher, help your teen perceive whatever they see in the media with critical eyes. Tell them the media, especially social media, is not always a reliable source of true information. Help them realize the folly of comparing themselves to idealized images they see online.
- Counter negative thinking with positive words of affirmation: Teens tend to be their worst critics and often beat themselves down when they are already at a low point. Whenever they make a negative statement about themselves, ask them to change their language

and tone to something more positive and rephrase the statement.

IN SUMMARY

In this chapter, we've explored stress in the lives of teenagers, starting with the definition and then discussing common stressors. If you've related to any of the stories presented, begin to use the tools and techniques laid out before you. Remember that revolutions demand radical change, do the work towards building your confidence! In the next chapter, you'll explore the art of setting goals and developing strategies to achieve your goals.

JOIN THE CONFIDENCE REVOLUTION!

UNLEASH YOUR GENEROSITY POWER

"The best way to find yourself is to lose yourself in the service of others."

— MAHATMA GANDHI

Hey there, amazing revolutionary reader! Are you finding value in the book so far?

Do you believe in the power of generosity? Well, guess what? You have a chance to make a real difference in someone's life, and it'll only take a minute of your time.

Imagine helping a fellow teenager overcome self-doubt, low self-esteem, and negativity. Picture them breaking free to pursue their dreams, express themselves, and interact with others. That's the potential impact of your review for Teen Confidence Revolution A Guide To Crush Negativity, Boost Self-Esteem, Reduce Stress, And Slay Your Goals! by Teen Powerhouse Society.

Our mission is to make this empowering book accessible to everyone, and we need your help. Your review can be the guiding light for someone who, just like you, is eager to make a positive change but might not know where to start.

Will you join us in this mission?

We believe that your generous act of leaving a review can transform lives. Your words could be the encouragement someone needs to:

- Build self-confidence and embrace their uniqueness.
- Manage stress and navigate the challenges of modern life.
- Set and achieve meaningful goals.
- Share the gift of confidence with others in their community.

Here's your chance to be part of a revolution that promotes positivity, growth, and support among teenagers. Your review is a small action that can lead to **big**, meaningful changes for someone out there.

Ready to spread the word?

It's easy! Simply visit [https://www.amazon.com/review/review-your-purchases/?asin=B0CSG5TLBH] to share your thoughts about the book.

By leaving a review, you're not just sharing your opinion; **you're contributing to a movement that empowers teens to reach their full potential.**

If you're on Audible Hit the three dots at the top right of your device click rate and review, then leave a few sentences about the book with a star rating.

If you are on Kindle or an eReader scroll to the bottom of the book then swipe up and it will prompt you to leave a review.

If for some reason these instructions do not work, simply go to Amazon or wherever you purchase the book and leave a review right on the books page. for Amazon, click here.

Thank you from the Teen Powerhouse Society!

Your generosity is valued beyond measure. We can't wait to continue this journey with you, unlocking more strategies to boost self-esteem, reduce stress, and help you achieve your goals.

Remember, your review isn't just about a book; it's about creating a ripple effect of confidence that can change lives. So, thank you for being a part of something incredible!

    Warm regards,
    Teen Powerhouse Society

PS - Share the positivity! If you know someone who could benefit from this book, send it their way and let's spread the Teen Confidence Revolution together.

Now its time to get YASSIFIED!

5

TIME TO GET YASSIFIED! GOAL SETTING FOR TEENS: DREAM BIG, ACHIEVE BIGGER

> *The world's greatest achievers have been those who have always stayed focused on their goals and have been consistent in their efforts.*
>
> — DR. ROOPLEEN

THE INSPIRING STORY OF LUNA FRANK, A COLLEGE JUNIOR

Luna Frank, a junior majoring in Social Work with a minor in Psychology, embarked on a path of self-discovery and growth. Initially, she set her sights on a career in law but later realized that her passion for social justice and how much she enjoyed helping out at the local youth center might make social work a better option. Her journey took an important turn when she met Damian Wyatt, a student advisor at her college, at a social justice event. Damian would become a crucial part of Luna's life.

For Luna, working with Damian wasn't just about academic guidance; it was about learning to prioritize and find balance in her life. She shared, "Damian has helped me to look at the bigger picture, to determine my vision for the future, and then see how each step I take fits into that vision." But one of the most transformative lessons Luna learned was the value of seeking help when needed. She admits that "Asking for help isn't always easy and it can be a pretty humbling experience but I wouldn't be where I am today without the help of others." She learned that it's perfectly acceptable to seek assistance when navigating life's complexities.

WHAT IS GOAL SETTING?

Goal setting is when you define what you want to achieve and outline the steps to get there. Just like an explorer setting out to conquer new territories, you, as a teenager, can set goals that lead to personal growth, success, and fulfillment.

For instance, your goal could be to learn a musical instrument, like the guitar, and eventually start a band with your friends. Imagine each practice session as a step toward hitting the right note on your adventure. Goal setting gives your dreams a direction, making them not just wishes but tangible destinations you can work toward. So, whether you aim to ace an exam, improve your soccer skills, or volunteer for a social cause, setting goals empowers you to navigate the exciting journey of your teenage life.

Teens: The Importance of Goal Setting

Goal setting has many advantages, here are some of the main ones:

- Direction and purpose: Goal setting provides you with a clear sense of direction in your life. It's like having a compass that points you toward your dreams. For instance, setting a goal to write a novel can motivate you to dedicate time to your craft every day, offering purpose and structure to your daily routine.
- Motivation and achievement: Goals act as your motivational boosters. When you set and achieve your goals, you experience a sense of accomplishment that fuels your self-esteem. For instance, setting a goal to improve your 2 mile run time by three minutes not only keeps you active but also builds your confidence as you hit that target.
- Focus and prioritization: Goal setting helps you prioritize your time and efforts. It helps you organize your to-do list and ensures the most important ones are at the top. As a student aiming to earn a merit scholarship, you may find it easier to make sure your homework, studies, and assignments get the most of your time and energy because you have a clear goal in mind.
- Resilience and adaptability: Working toward goals cultivates resilience and adaptability. Just like an athlete adjusts their game plan in response to changing weather conditions, you learn to adapt to life's

challenges. For example, setting a goal to learn a new language and challenging yourself to speak it in public with native speakers, helps you build courage and persistence to strengthen resilience and adaptability.
- Empowerment and self-discovery: Goal setting empowers you to take charge of your life. It's like giving you the keys to a car; you get to decide where you want to go. For instance, setting a goal to try something new every month allows you to discover where your passions lie.

GOAL-SETTING THEORIES AND TOOLS

In the world of goal setting, there are fascinating theories that dive into the science behind setting and achieving our ambitions. These theories offer valuable insights into how our minds work and provide practical strategies for making our dreams a reality. In the following section, we'll explore some intriguing theories, each with a unique perspective on how to set and reach the goals that matter most to you.

The Locke-Latham Goal Setting Theory

The Locke-Latham goal-setting theory, pioneered by Dr. Edwin Locke and Dr. Gary Latham, provides valuable insights into the art of goal-setting. The Locke-Latham duo found that, in fostering high task performance, merely encouraging individuals to do their best is less effective than establishing specific and challenging goals (Latham & Locke, 2007).

Imagine you aim to improve your grades. Instead of just saying, "I want better grades," applying the Locke-Latham theory would mean setting a specific goal, like, "I will raise my math grade from a C to an A by the end of the semester." Do you notice how the specific details create a clear target to work towards? This makes your goals more motivating and actionable.

Moreover, the theory encourages breaking down your goals into smaller, manageable steps. If your goal is to explore your fascination with languages, you can start by setting a specific, challenging objective like, "I will learn to speak a new language in three months." You can break your main goal into smaller milestones such as learning five new phrases a week. The Locke-Latham theory shows that achieving these mini-goals along the way not only boosts your motivation but also builds confidence and a sense of accomplishment. Applying this theory means setting specific, challenging goals, and breaking them into smaller steps.

SMARTER Goals and How to Set Them

SMARTER is an acronym that acts as a helpful guide for setting goals. It stands for Specific, Measurable, Attainable, Realistic, Time-bound, Evaluate, and Reward. Each of these elements plays a crucial role in turning your dreams into tangible, achievable objectives. By following the SMARTER criteria, you can make your ambitions clear, practical, and motivating, ensuring your journey to success is marked by focus and direction.

- **(S)pecific:** Your goal should be crystal clear and specific. When your goal lacks specificity, you might feel lost or overwhelmed. For example, instead of saying, "I want to be better at basketball," a specific goal would be, "I want to improve my dribbling skills in basketball." This clarity helps you focus on the exact area that you want to improve.
- **(M)easurable:** Make sure you can track your progress. It's challenging to stay motivated if you don't have a way to measure your progress. For example, instead of saying, "I want to read more," you could set a measurable goal like, "I want to read one book every month." Measuring your progress helps you stay on track and celebrate small victories.
- **(A)ttainable:** Your goal should be something you can achieve based on your abilities and resources. Setting goals that are beyond your reach can lead to frustration and disappointment. For instance, if you're new to running, setting a goal to run a marathon within the first month might not be realistic. A more attainable goal could be to complete a 5K race in four months. This ensures that your goals push you without overwhelming you.
- **(R)ealistic:** Your goal should align with your life and priorities. Unrealistic goals can lead to burnout and neglect of other important aspects of your life. If you have a busy school schedule and various extracurricular activities, a goal like practicing the guitar for three hours every day might not be realistic. A more realistic

goal could be to practice for 30 minutes each day. Realistic goals ensure you maintain a healthy balance.
- **(T)ime-bound:** Your goal should have a deadline. Without a timeline, your goal may remain a distant dream. For example, instead of saying, "I'll learn to paint someday," set a time-bound goal like, "I'll complete my first painting within two months." This time constraint spurs you into consistent action, avoiding procrastination.
- **(E)valuate:** By evaluating your goals daily, you significantly increase your chances of achieving them. Why? Because long-term goals can easily slip from your focus if you don't evaluate them regularly. Set up a reliable system for daily goal evaluation, and make it a habit.
- **(R)eward**: By offering yourself something to look forward to, like seeing a movie or going to a concert, you stay committed to your journey, maintaining focus and consistency. A well-defined reward system ensures you have a positive outcome to strive for.

By crafting SMARTER goals, you're not just setting yourself up for success, but you're also ensuring that your journey toward your dreams is clear, motivating, and enjoyable, while avoiding common pitfalls like aimlessness, frustration, burnout, and procrastination.

The PACT vs SMARTER Goals

While SMARTER is a great goal-making theory, there is an alternative method. PACT, like SMARTER, is a theory that guides the goal-setting process, but with a different focus. Let's look at PACT, how it compares to SMARTER, and which theory you should use.

Introducing PACT

In your journey of setting and achieving goals, you may come across the PACT theory. PACT stands for "Purposeful, Actionable, Continuous, and Trackable." This goal-setting approach introduces a unique perspective that emphasizes the significance of adding meaning and depth to your goals.

PACT vs SMARTER: Differences in Focus

Now, let's compare PACT with the well-known SMARTER approach and explore the differences in their focus and application. While both theories share a common emphasis on creating actionable goals, PACT takes it a step further by incorporating the crucial element of "purpose."

In the context of academic improvement, a traditional SMARTER goal might look like, "I will achieve straight A grades this semester." However, a PACT goal would encompass a deeper purpose, such as, "I aim to purposefully excel in my studies to lay a strong foundation for a successful future." This additional layer of purpose encourages you to connect your goals with your core values and long-term aspirations, making them more motivational.

Should You Use PACT or SMARTER?

If you have specific, measurable targets and prefer a straightforward approach, SMARTER might be more suitable. However, if you want to infuse your goals with a deeper sense of purpose, make them part of a continuous journey, and enhance your overall motivation, PACT could be the ideal choice. Ultimately, you can use both tools depending on the nature of your goals. Don't be afraid to use multiple tools.

The WOOP Goal Setting Tool

The WOOP tool is a newcomer in the realm of goal setting, yet it draws on over two decades of research (Difference Psychology, 2022). This approach blends the power of positive thinking with the skills of visualization and preparing for potential obstacles on your journey.

- **(W)ish:** Begin by identifying your wish, or your desired outcome. Imagine something you want to achieve, like improving your grades in school, becoming a better athlete, getting a summer job, or learning to cook a meal. For example, your wish might be, "I want to excel in my upcoming exams," "I want to learn to cook a complete meal" or "I want to get a great summer job."
- **(O)utcome:** The next step is to envision the positive outcome or result you'd experience if you achieved your wish. This helps to reinforce your motivation. In the context of academic goals, the outcome could be, "If I excel in my exams, I'll feel proud of my

accomplishments and have more opportunities for future success."
- **(O)bstacle:** Recognize the potential obstacles that might stand in your way. These could include procrastination, distractions, or self-doubt. Identifying obstacles prepares you to deal with challenges proactively.
- **(P)lan:** Finally, create a detailed plan to overcome the obstacles and work towards your wish. If procrastination is an obstacle, your plan could involve setting a study schedule, eliminating distractions, and using time-management techniques to stay on track. This approach helps you take tangible steps toward your goal and navigate any roadblocks that come your way.

HARD Goal Setting Tool

HARD goals are audacious, demanding, and, as the name suggests, hard. It's designed to push you to your limits and make your wildest dreams a reality. Imagine this scenario: You recently broke your leg in several places. But your aspirations go beyond just walking again; you're not satisfied with the ordinary. What you aim for is to regain your full mobility and then go a step further—to run in the renowned Boston Marathon. HARD goals push your limits and invite you to explore the potential within you.

The HARD goal-setting tool encourages you to create goals that are emotionally charged, clearly visualized, supported by necessary routines, and challenging enough to drive your personal growth and success (Murphy, 2011).

- **(H)eartfelt:** Your goals should be deeply meaningful and emotionally connected to you. When you set heartfelt goals, they are driven by genuine passion and commitment.
- **(A)nimated**: Emphasizes being able to vividly visualize your success. You should be able to see yourself accomplishing your goals, which can be a powerful motivator.
- **(R)equired**: Highlights the routines and actions necessary to achieve your goals. It's essential to identify and implement the specific steps and habits required for success.
- **(D)ifficult**: Suggests that your goals should be challenging. By setting ambitious objectives, you push yourself to the limit and continue to grow in your higher potential.

GOAL-SETTING TIPS

No matter which goal-setting strategy you decide to use, here are some tips that can help you succeed.

- **Break it down:** Breaking down your goals into manageable steps allows you to create a roadmap for success. You'll have a clearer understanding of where to start and how to proceed, making your main goal seem less daunting. Outline specific actions you need to take for each step to ensure a smooth journey.

- **Learn to say no:** Prioritizing your goals may require setting boundaries. Politely decline offers or opportunities that might divert your attention from your goals. Remember that saying "no" in one instance is often saying "yes" to your dreams and aspirations.
- **Reward yourself:** Acknowledging your accomplishments along the way can keep you motivated. Define rewards that are meaningful to you and tie them to specific milestones. It could be a favorite treat, or even time spent playing a video game you enjoy. These small celebrations can fuel your determination.
- **Be patient with yourself:** Understand that big dreams often take time to realize. Be patient and compassionate with yourself during challenging times or periods of slower progress. Keeping your eye on the forest instead of a single fallen tree helps you stay committed to the journey.
- **Learn from setbacks:** Embrace setbacks as opportunities to learn and grow. Analyze what went wrong, the factors involved, and how you can adapt your strategy to avoid similar hurdles in the future. Setbacks become stepping stones to success when you view them as lessons.
- **Visualize your success:** Visualization involves creating mental images of your accomplished goal. This technique can help you maintain focus and belief in

your goals. Regularly picture yourself achieving what you've set out to do, as this fosters confidence.
- **Find an accountability partner:** Share your goals with someone you trust, whether it's a friend, family member, or mentor. They can help hold you accountable and provide support, encouragement, and advice along the way.
- **Regularly review your goals:** Every now and again, assess your goals to ensure they remain aligned with your current aspirations. Adjust them as needed to reflect your changing priorities or new opportunities that may arise.
- **Prioritize self-care:** To sustain the energy and resilience you need to pursue your goals, you will need to take good care of your physical and mental well-being. Ensure you get enough rest, eat healthy foods, exercise, and manage your stress effectively.
- **Seek feedback:** Always welcome feedback from others, as it can provide you with fresh insights and guidance. Collaborate with mentors, coaches, or peers who can offer valuable suggestions, critique, or encouragement to help refine your approach.

PARENTS/TEACHERS: HOW TO SUPPORT YOUR TEEN'S GOALS

The first thing on your checklist should be to make sure that your teen's goals are truly their own. Evaluate how much influence you've had over their goal-setting process. If you're the mastermind behind all their goals and plans, there's a chance they'll lack the passion and drive to overcome challenges they might encounter in pursuit of their goals. As your teen nears adulthood, more of their decisions should be aligned with their own passions, aspirations, interests, dreams, and talents. By stepping back and allowing your teen to steer their own course, you're allowing them to free themselves from the desire to please you, and discover their own passions.

After affirming that your teen has set their goals based on what they truly want, become their partners in accomplishing it. Support them in overcoming challenges, respectfully guide and advise them on the best path to take, and offer a supportive ear when they need to vent. Choosing to support your teen is not about approving of their goals, but about showing that you respect them enough to make their own decisions and are willing to let their process of self-discovery take place.

As part of supporting them, regularly remind your teens of the power they have in the course of their own destinies. Sometimes, your teen may vent about something they don't like, for instance, their weight. Kindly remind them that while you empathize with them for the frustration they are experiencing, the good news is that they have the power to achieve a healthier weight. In some cases, teens face challenges they have no control over. In such cases, point out that while they can't control the situation, they can control their attitude towards it.

Explain to your teen that the person they become as a result of successfully striving toward their goals is more important than the accomplishment of the goal itself. To achieve their goals, they end up exercising a good degree of resilience, consistency, hard work, and determination. In striving for their goals, they will obtain these qualities and positively impact everything else they endeavor. This quote by Henry David Thoreau sums this up nicely, "What you get by achieving your goals is not as important as what you become by achieving your goals."

PRACTICAL TOOL: CHOOSE ONE OF THE TOOLS BELOW

Below you'll find each goal-setting tool covered in this chapter. Use one or all of the tools below and see what works best for you.

SMARTER Goals:

What is your goal?

- **S**pecific: Clearly break down exactly what you want to improve or achieve, use numbers if possible.
- **M**easurable: How will you measure your progress toward your goal?
- **A**ttainable: How attainable is your goal, considering your current resources such as time, and energy?
- **R**ealistic: How realistic is your goal, with regard to your current priorities?
- **T**ime: What is the deadline for your goal?
- **E**valuate: What progress have you made so far?
- **R**eward: How will you reward your progress or achievements?

PACT Goals:

What is your goal?

- **P**urpose: Why is this goal important to you?
- **A**ctionable: What specific actions will you take to achieve this goal?
- **C**ontinuous: How will you make consistent progress?
- **T**rackable: How will you measure your progress and success?

WOOP Goals

- **W**ish: What is your wish or desired outcome?
- **O**utcome: What will be the best outcome if you achieve your goal?
- **O**bstacle: What obstacles or challenges might you encounter?
- **P**lan: How will you overcome those obstacles and make your goal a reality?

HARD Goals

- **H**eartfelt: How emotionally invested are you in this goal?
- **A**nimated: Can you vividly envision yourself succeeding?
- **R**equired: What routines and actions are required for success?

- **Difficult:** How challenging is this goal? What pushes your limits?

IN SUMMARY

In this chapter, we've explored goal setting and gained a deep understanding of its importance. We looked at practical tips for crafting attainable goals, various goal-setting theories, and effective strategies, and finally completed a goal-setting worksheet activity. Your journey to goal accomplishment is exciting but you will likely encounter some obstacles along the way. Don't worry because the process of setting and achieving goals is inherently linked to resilience, the subject of our next chapter.

6

BE BAD AND BOUJEE: OVERCOMING OBSTACLES AND RESILIENCE

> *Resilience is accepting your new reality, even if it's less good than the one you had before. You can fight it, you can do nothing but scream about what you've lost, or you can accept that and try to put together something that's good.*
>
> — ELIZABETH EDWARDS

A STORY OF TEEN RESILIENCE: AZIZA, A YOUNG VOLUNTEER IN GHANA

Aziza, a dedicated young volunteer, embarked on a mission to find a safe, easy way to get to school. When she started high school, she discovered that more of her classmates were reluctant to go to school, since it was a much further trip than before. Most people in her community couldn't afford to pay for private transport and there were no that add depth and color to your life story, providing you with tales worth sharing and celebrating. In contrast, a journey without challenges may seem monotonous and lacks the exciting chapters that make your story truly remarkable.

OBSTACLES TO EMBRACING CHALLENGES

Even though embracing challenges has many benefits, there are obstacles that may stand in your way. Below we explore four ways why you may struggle to accept challenges as an opportunity for growth and a normal part of your life and how to reframe your thinking to better deal with adversity.

Thinking That Seeking Help Is a Display of Vulnerability

Instead of thinking that seeking help is a sign of vulnerability, consider it a demonstration of your wisdom and self-awareness. Know that no one has all the answers, which means that asking for help is an act of courage and a clear sign of your commitment to personal growth and continuous improvement.

Doubting Your Worthiness of Support and Assistance

Shift your mindset from doubting your worthiness to acknowledging that everyone deserves support when faced with challenges. Just as you'd readily offer help to a friend, trust that your needs are just as valid. When you open up and let friends be there for you, it not only strengthens the bond you share but also allows them to experience the joy of supporting you.

Waiting for Others to Offer Help First

Rather than waiting for others to take the initiative, understand that you have the power to actively seek assistance. By being proactive, you take control of your journey, demonstrating leadership and a commitment to overcoming obstacles. If you don't ask for help, how will people know you need assistance?

Surrendering to Challenges Too Quickly

Instead of giving up in haste, remind yourself that challenges are an opportunity for growth. Embrace them as a chance to learn, adapt, and emerge stronger, recognizing that perseverance is often the key to ultimate success. Have faith that you'll never encounter a challenge too great for you to overcome.

BUILDING RESILIENCE: STRATEGIES FOR SUCCESS

Resilience is the capacity we have to adapt and thrive when confronting challenges, threats, or significant stressors. We can also view resilience as the natural ability we have to float back up to the surface after being repeatedly pushed under by life's toughest moments. Developing resilience can mean the difference between coping with and overcoming these challenges or allowing them to negatively define your entire life.

What Resilience Looks Like

As a resilient teen, you will have the following characteristics:

- Emotional awareness and regulation: You can recognize when you're feeling overwhelmed or anxious and use techniques like deep breathing or mindfulness to regain your composure.
- Impulse control: When faced with the temptation to procrastinate or engage in impulsive behaviors, you're more likely to resist these urges, enabling you to stay on track with your responsibilities.
- Optimistic outlook: Even in the face of challenges, you maintain a positive attitude, believing that you can improve with hard work and dedication.
- Flexible and accurate thinking: You can view problems from multiple perspectives and think critically, which helps you find creative solutions to complex issues.
- Empathy towards others: You're empathetic and understanding, offering support to friends who are struggling and actively listening to their concerns.
- Self-efficacy: You believe in your capabilities. For instance, you tackle a challenging project with confidence, knowing you have the skills to succeed.
- Willingness to seek help: When facing personal difficulties, you have the courage to reach out to trusted adults, such as a parent or a school mentor, for guidance and support.

THE LINK BETWEEN A GROWTH MINDSET AND GREATER RESILIENCE

When you have a growth mindset, you believe that intelligence, skills, and talents can be developed and improved over time through dedication. You embrace challenges, persist in the face of setbacks, see effort as a path to mastery, and learn from criticism (Kristenson, 2022a). You view failures as learning opportunities and understand that success is not solely determined by your natural abilities but also by your hard work and putting into practice what you learn.

For example, when you receive a poor grade on a math test, a growth mindset helps you believe that you can improve your math skills through practice and seeking help. You see the low grade as a sign that you need to give more attention, and you don't feel discouraged. This mindset motivates you to study more and ask questions, and eventually, your math scores improve.

On the other hand, when you have a fixed mindset, you believe that abilities are innate and unchangeable. You tend to avoid challenges, give up easily in the face of setbacks, and ignore useful feedback (Machina, 2022). You believe that your success or failure is determined by your inherent talent, and you fear that putting in effort is a sign of incompetence.

For instance, consider you receive a low grade on a science project. If you have a fixed mindset, you may think you're simply "not good at science." You won't see the value in studying more or seeking help because you believe you're naturally incapable. Having this mindset can lead to a lack of resilience and an unwillingness to tackle future challenges.

Resilience is closely tied to a growth mindset because it encourages you to persevere, adapt, and keep trying, even in the face of adversity. When you develop a growth mindset, you become more resilient because you understand that setbacks are opportunities for growth and that you have the power to overcome obstacles through effort and practice.

But if you have a fixed mindset, it can be tough to bounce back from setbacks. Challenges might seem too daunting, and you may not want to put in the effort to overcome them because you believe you can't change that much.

A fixed mindset can hold you back because it makes you shy away from challenges and doubt your abilities to grow and overcome. Developing a growth mindset can boost your ability to be resilient. It empowers you to embrace challenges, learn from them, and keep going, no matter what.

Parents/Teachers: How You Can Help Your Teen Develop a Growth Mindset

To foster a growth mindset in your teen, avoid praising them solely for being smart or talented. Instead, celebrate their efforts when they tackle challenges and employ effective strategies. Praising intelligence alone might inadvertently nurture a fixed mindset, hindering their potential for growth. Encourage them to understand that it's okay to sometimes grapple with tough problems before seeking assistance, as these struggles are opportunities for them to grasp new concepts and enhance their problem-solving abilities.

Present them with tasks that are challenging but not overwhelming; this approach can enhance their performance in various areas. Additionally, let your teen know that you believe in their ability to overcome difficulties and learn from their mistakes. Teach them to replace "I can't" with "I can't yet," conveying how the brain forms new connections as they learn.

By implementing these strategies, you're helping your teen develop a growth mindset, allowing them to embrace challenges, persist in the face of setbacks, and view effort as a path to mastery. These qualities will not only enhance their academic performance but also equip them with essential life skills, ultimately building their resiliency.

Tips to Help Build Resilience

Talk to People

When you talk to people you get to express yourself, listen to advice, and ask questions. By sharing your experiences with parents, friends, social networks, or religious groups, you can process your feelings, find comfort in knowing you're not alone, and feel heard and understood. Seeking advice and insights from those with more life experience can offer valuable perspectives. Engaging in conversations and actively seeking help or advice demonstrates resilience and a commitment to personal growth.

Give Yourself a Break

During difficult situations or tragedies, the everyday stresses you experience can feel even more overwhelming. Not to mention your emotions are already in turmoil because of hormonal shifts and the physical changes that come with adolescence. In such moments, make sure that you're understanding and compassionate towards yourself and your friends. Recognize that these ups and downs are a natural part of growing up, and it's perfectly fine to step back, take a deep breath, and give yourself or your friends some space and understanding.

Sometimes No News Is Good News

It's good to stay informed, especially when you have homework that requires you to follow the news. However, make sure to strike a balance. The news often tends to focus on sensational or negative stories, which can contribute to the feeling that everything is going wrong. To manage your stress, consider controlling the amount of news you consume. Whether you get your news from television, newspapers, magazines, or the Internet, try to set reasonable limits.

Regain Sight of the Bigger Picture

In times of stress, it's essential to maintain perspective. Remember that the source of your stress won't be relevant forever; things change, and difficult times eventually pass. Remind yourself of past experiences when you faced fears or overcame challenges, as a way to remind yourself of your inner strength. Practice relaxation techniques, such as visualizing a peaceful place or taking deep breaths to calm down. Focus on the aspects of life that remain constant amid changing circumstances.

Parents/Teachers: Tips to Support Your Teen in Building Resilience

The 7 C's —Competence, Confidence, Connection, Character, Contribution, Coping, and Control—form the foundation of resilience (Hurley, 2022). As a parent or teacher, you can help your teenager strengthen these, thereby strengthening their resilience. Use the following tips to guide your active involvement in supporting your teen in developing each of the seven C's.

Competence

Share with your teen that perfection is an unattainable goal. Guide them to set realistic goals and remind them to add the word "yet" when they feel they "can't do something." Share stories of your own imperfections and how they've contributed to your personal growth. Help them understand that competence is a journey, a continuous work in progress!

Confidence

Remind your teen that grades alone don't define their identity or their entire future. Many colleges take a holistic approach to admissions, choosing not to focus solely on GPA. One poor grade isn't a roadblock; it's a chance to learn and grow. Encourage them not to lose hope or confidence, as their potential is not limited by a solitary setback.

Connection

In this case, connection means the feeling of belonging.

Support your teens in developing their independence by giving them opportunities to spend time with friends with relatively little supervision. Allowing them to socialize with friends without constant adult oversight helps them build stronger connections with peers and equips them with valuable relationship skills for their adulthood.

Character

Assist your teens in managing stress, as stress can sometimes lead them to lose sight of their core values. Equipping them with effective stress-coping strategies will enable them to preserve and enhance the strong character necessary for resilience.

Contribution

Encourage your teen to actively participate in family and class engagements, demonstrating that their opinions are seen as important. Taking their input seriously and engaging in open discussions, even when decisions go a different way, helps them take ownership of their choices and fosters resilience and responsibility.

Coping

Discuss the concept of mindfulness as a coping strategy. Emphasize that mindfulness practices can help them regain composure and focus. Support your teen in discovering a mindfulness activity that can assist them in managing stressful situations effectively.

Control

Assist your teen in establishing goals and planning strategies to provide a sense of direction, enabling them to stay focused even when facing unforeseen challenges. Encourage them to set their own objectives, so that they have a greater sense of control and reduce the likelihood of disappointment if things don't go as planned.

Practical Journal Exercises For Building Resilience Through Growth Mindset

Embracing Challenges

1. Think about a challenge you've faced recently (e.g., a difficult school project, or a personal goal).
2. Write down how you initially felt about the challenge. Did you see it as an opportunity to learn and grow, or did you feel overwhelmed?
3. Now, reflect on how you can view this challenge with a growth mindset. How can you turn it into a learning experience? Write down your thoughts.

Mistakes and Learning

1. Recall a time when you made a mistake or didn't succeed at something. Write down what happened and how you felt.

2. Now, think about what you learned from that experience. Did it teach you anything valuable?
   3. Write down how you can apply what you learned from that mistake to future challenges.

Positive Self-Talk

   1. List three common negative thoughts you might have about yourself or your abilities.
   2. For each negative thought, write a positive and growth-oriented counter-thought. For example, if you think, "I'm not good at math," you can reframe it as "I can improve my math skills with practice and effort."

Goal Setting

   1. Set a specific goal you want to achieve. It could be related to school, a hobby, or personal development.
   2. Break down your goal into smaller, achievable steps. This will help you measure your progress.
   3. Write down how having a growth mindset will help you work toward and achieve this goal.

The Power of "Yet"

   1. Think about something you're not good at right now, but you'd like to improve. It could be a skill, a subject, or a hobby.

2. Write down that area of improvement, and then add "yet" to the end. For example, if you're not a great guitar player, write, "I'm not a great guitar player... yet."
3. Reflect on how this simple addition of "yet" changes your perspective and encourages you to keep trying and learning.

Parents/Teachers: A Resilience Building Activity

Achieving success in life is closely tied to our ability to take calculated risks and navigate fears. Here's a list of daring activities to consider letting your teenager explore to help build resilience.

- Traveling, alone or in a group: Depending on their age and experience, suggest that your teen travels solo or with a group of friends, even if it's just on a weekend getaway.
- Zip-lining or hot-air balloon ride: These experiences force teens to face their fears head-on. While the risks are well-managed in these activities, the experience will be life-changing.
- Wilderness survival camp: These programs expose teens to challenging outdoor situations, teaching them basic survival skills, navigation, and self-reliance. Under the guidance of experts, they'll learn to build shelter, make fires, and find food and water in the wild.
- Cultural exchange programs: If possible, sign your teen up for a cultural exchange program where they can live with a host family in a foreign country. It will be an

eye-opening experience that fosters adaptability and independence.
- Rock climbing: Rock climbing will challenge your teen both physically and mentally. As they face frightening heights and tackle difficult routes, they're guaranteed to learn essential life skills such as problem-solving, risk management, and the value of teamwork.

IN SUMMARY

Resilience is a powerful skill that enables you to navigate life's challenges and emerge stronger. Your confidence toolkit now includes practical strategies you can use to build resilience and its role in fostering adaptability and personal growth. Parents and educators understand the value of allowing teens to have more freedom to learn because by encouraging teens to explore more of life's experiences, parents help teens add to the arsenal of tools that reinforce resilience. In the next chapter, we'll talk about friends and their contribution to your happiness and why true connection matters to your overall well-being.

7

CREATING A CONFIDENCE REVOLUTION COMMUNITY: YOUR SUPPORT NETWORK

> *Think back to the most important experiences of your life, the highest highs, the greatest victories, the most daunting obstacles overcome. How many happened to you alone? I bet there are very few. When you understand that being connected to others is one of life's greatest joys, you realize that life's best comes when you initiate and invest in solid relationships.*
>
> — JOHN C. MAXWELL

TWO SISTERS HARNESS THE POWER OF COMMUNITY

Meet Annabelle and Aurora, two amazing sisters who have started their very own foundation. They believe that everyone can give back and positively impact their community, just like they did.

Annabelle started volunteering in her community when she was in 5th grade and has already spent over 800 hours giving back. Her sister Aurora is just as passionate about volunteering. Together, they formed a foundation with a mission to work with communities, provide volunteer and leadership opportunities, and spread kindness.

Their efforts to connect with people in the community helped them expand their reach and impact. By involving the community, they managed to serve over 9 homeless shelters, offer tutoring to children in 15 different schools, and provide over 4,000 books to underprivileged kids. The bonds formed within the community strengthened their foundation and enabled them to achieve more together.

Together with the power of community, perhaps another secret to Annabelle and Aurora's success, lies in their friendship. Their shared passion for giving back and their mutual support fueled their efforts. Their friendship became a source of resilience and motivation, showing us that when friends share a common purpose, they can accomplish incredible feats.

THE POWER OF CONNECTION

Social connections are basically the relationships and interactions that you have with your peers, trusted adults, and the community. These connections provide you with a sense of belonging, support, and the opportunity to share experiences. They are transformative, influencing your identity, emotional well-being, and personal growth, ultimately helping you to thrive during your adolescent years.

The Importance of Building Social Connections

A Beacon of Light at the End of the Tunnel

When you're facing a challenge, your social connections can be a source of solace and resilience. These connections are more than just a way to share laughter and companionship; they serve as a crucial support system, especially when times get tough.

Imagine you've been struggling with a school project that is starting to feel like an unsolvable puzzle. You're feeling overwhelmed, and it seems like you've hit a dead end. However, after a chat with a friend, you start to see your project from a new angle. Your friend's point of view and ideas bring fresh solutions you hadn't thought of before. This is the power that lies in talking through your challenges with others and using them as a sounding board to gain a fresh perspective.

In times of hurt or crisis, it can often feel like the pain is never-ending. You may find yourself thinking, "I can't take this anymore." In moments like this, a reassuring voice that says, "You will get through this," can mean the difference between surrendering to despair and finding the strength to persevere. It's a reminder that you're not alone in your struggle.

The journey of life is filled with unexpected twists and turns. Many teens before you have walked similar paths and made the same mistakes you fear you might make. When someone who's been through your current situation shares their wisdom, it can help you avoid unnecessary pitfalls. So, instead of personally going through every trial and error, through social connections, you can learn from others' experiences. As part of a community, seeing others holding onto hope can also help reinforce your own and strengthen your resolve.

In essence, by nurturing social connections you can build relationships that offer support, wisdom, hope, and a renewed sense of purpose. They remind you that true and caring relationships make a difference in your journey. When you have a community that is ready to stand by your side, it helps you to build your confidence.

Your Support Network: The Power of Friendship

Friends Help You Cope With Stress

During your teen years, your friendships can be a lifeline when you're dealing with tough situations. A study from 2021 found that having strong friendships before the pandemic helped teens handle the stress of isolation and social distancing. These connections made a big difference by helping to reduce feelings of loneliness, depression, and anxiety.

Apart from life-changing events such as the pandemic, your friends are there for you when you face everyday stress, such as failing a test, getting through a disagreement with a parent, or dealing with a challenging school project. You might even cope better with stress when you're with your friends, not adults. Being with your peers can lower feelings of sadness, jealousy, and anxiety, highlighting just how important peer connections can be for a teen.

Besides having support during stressful or tough times, what are the other ways that being in a community beats isolation?

- Strong immune system: Teens with robust social connections might have a better ability to fight off illnesses since being part of a community helps you stay healthier and more energized.
- Boosted self-esteem: Having friends who appreciate and support you can do wonders for your self-esteem. For example, hearing your friends cheer you on during band practice or a debate competition can make you feel more confident—like you're already a winner.
- Reduced anxiety: Adolescent friendships are like a natural stress reliever. Chatting with your friends about your worries and sharing a laugh, relaxes you and eases your anxiety.
- Happiness and optimism: Being part of a community tends to make you happier and more optimistic. When you have friends to share fun moments and challenges with, it brightens your outlook on life. Your community can turn an ordinary day into a memorable adventure, and the joy of sharing exciting news with friends makes it all the sweeter!

Parents/Teachers: How to Help Your Teen Connect

It can be deeply worrying to see your teen struggling with isolation and loneliness. It hurts to see them struggling without the joy and fulfillment that friendships can bring. You know your teen is an amazing kid, they have interesting quirks, talents, and abilities. They may be really smart, funny, and empathic. You wish you could help in some way, but you don't know how. Luckily there are ways you can help move them closer to making their next friend. Let's unpack some very practical ways you can help your teen step out of isolation and build connections with others.

Don't force them to do things they're not interested in. Going out and taking part in activities is a great way to meet like-minded people who may become potential friends. This is why it's best if you encourage your teen to participate in activities that they find interesting. Perhaps they're a fan of classic drama, and up until now have been satisfied with just reading and writing plays. Encourage them to join a drama club, this can spark conversations with peers who share their interests and ultimately cultivate friendships.

Most children learn how to interpret social cues and use them to convey meaning by the time they reach adolescence. However, if your teen seems oblivious to social cues, and unaware of what body language conveys, it could be the reason why they struggle to make friends. Explain to your teen that others use non-verbal cues like posture, facial expression, tone of voice, and eye contact to gauge their potential interest or readiness for social interaction. If they are inadvertently giving off negative 'stay away' signals, potential friends won't ever approach them or will do so with caution. Tell them that smiling, laughing, and making eye contact always let others know you are open to engaging.

Help teens understand the power of showing a genuine interest in others. Teens who tend to be alone sometimes spend most of their time in their heads. They often find their imaginary world far more colorful and interesting than the real world. Many people have active imaginations but still manage to be mentally present and find joy in making meaningful connections in real life. Just like the characters in a novel, every person has their own background story. Ignite in them an interest to get to know people, and to learn more about their stories, for the joy of it.

CREATE YOUR TEEN CONFIDENCE REVOLUTION COMMUNITY

The social bonds you form with other people can vary in closeness and familiarity. You might have close connections with family, friends, classmates, or co-workers, or more distant ones with acquaintances. Some connections are as near as your next-door neighbor, while others might be geographically distant, but maintained through phone calls or online interactions. Regardless of the size of your social circle, what truly matters is that you're there for one another.

While some social connections might initially seem appealing, they may not align with your values or priorities. For instance, the person might pressure you to experiment with drugs or alcohol when you know it's not good for you, or they may not offer the support you need in crucial moments. It's perfectly okay to seek out other friends instead who provide a positive and supportive environment that resonates with your goals and well-being.

Importance of Social Connections

Positive social connections play a vital role in shaping your life, adding a sense of meaning and purpose to your journey. When you actively give and receive support within your chosen community, your life becomes more fulfilling.

Furthermore, these connections act as a protective shield, helping you to enhance your resilience and bounce back from tough situations or challenges. They contribute to your overall happiness, fostering a positive outlook and boosting your well-being. It's reassuring to know that in times of difficulty, you can lean on the strength of your community to provide support and a reassuring sense of stability.

How to Start Your Own Support Network

Enough waiting around, hoping that by a stroke of luck, you'll be invited into an existing community. What if they're not into the stuff you're into? Who's in charge of starting communities anyway, why can't that be you? Bringing together a group of people with similar interests is exciting and rewarding. Read the following steps to start your own community and just go for it!

Step One: Determine the Goal

So, you've decided to start your own community. Before you start sending out personal invites, think about what the purpose of your community will be. Do you want to become camping buddies, a tennis club, or something spiritual like a bible study group?

Step Two: Send Out Personal Invites

Now, it's time to assemble your dream team. Who are the people who inspire you to be a better version of yourself? Take a moment to think about it—and then reach out to them. Send out some invites and make sure you explain your vision for the community. Keep it cozy; bigger isn't always better. Aim for a tight-knit group of 5-10 people. Quality over quantity, always.

Step Three: Determine a Regular Meeting Time

Consistency is the name of the game, but life can get hectic. Check everyone's schedules and be realistic about how often you can meet. Once a week? Great. Once a month? Totally cool. The key is to stick to your schedule. If you don't make a pact as a group and commit to these meet-ups, your newly-found group will eventually disband.

Step Four: Find a Program That Fits Your Goal

Remember that goal you decided on in Step One? Time to back it up with the right program. Here are some examples:

- Growing in friendship: Dedicate an hour to your meeting. Spend the first 15 minutes socializing—

possibly with snacks or a game. Use the next 30 to share your "highs and lows" of the week. Finish up with 15 minutes to discuss personal stories or challenges.
- Growing in mutual support: Choose a new topic to discuss at each meeting that helps your community bond. Maybe it could be related to books, movies, or hobbies you all enjoy.
- Growing in understanding life: Pick a book or discussion topic to explore together. Make sure it's something that interests everyone in the group.

Step Five: Commit to That Program

Whatever your community's mission, give it your all. Just like a plant needs water, your community needs commitment and care. Show up to your meetings, and make an effort to nurture the individual relationships within your group.

Step Six: Evaluate, Make Adjustments, and Keep Going

Simple, right? But don't forget to check in with your community regularly. If things seem a bit off, don't hesitate to ask for feedback. Keep at it, you've got this!

IN SUMMARY

As we wrap up this chapter, it's crucial to remember that building social connections isn't just a part of life; it's an essential foundation for your well-being and overall happiness. You now know that a network of friends offers you support, companionship, and a sense of belonging. It's in these connections that you'll find comfort in both good times and bad, and the people who'll cheer you on and lift you up. You'll learn, grow, and share experiences, forming lasting memories with those who appreciate you for who you are.

Teens who are enthusiastically engaged in creating a community of their own can enhance their lives and ultimately build a group of like-minded peers who share in their goals and passions. That is what we will discuss in the next chapter, It's time to pursue your dreams!

8

UNLEASH THE BADDIE: UNLOCK YOUR PASSIONS AND DREAMS

> *Passion is one great force that unleashes creativity, because if you're passionate about something, then you're more willing to take risks.*
>
> — YO-YO MA

A STORY OF TEEN DREAMERS

Yumna and Zain are two teens who joined a group of young volunteers in their neighborhood to revive a neglected public park. When they realized that their cherished childhood place needed a breath of new life, they reached out to their local youth organization for help. Yumna emphasized how important this has been for her: "I have so many good memories here and I feel obligated to give back".

With some support from their local municipality, they planted trees, cleaned the park, and painted the seats and signs. Everyone in the community came together, driven by their shared desire to offer a free space for local families to gather, as Zain explained, "For many children, the park is the only place in the neighborhood where they can come to play and meet their friends."

Through their dedicated efforts, these young volunteers illustrate the transformative power of passion and community engagement, turning a negative situation into something beautiful. Their commitment to revitalizing a beloved park exemplifies how passion and dedication can be the drivers of change.

WHAT IS PASSION, AND HOW IS IT SIGNIFICANT?

Passion is the intense drive and enthusiasm that pushes you to pursue something wholeheartedly. It's the genuine, unwavering dedication to a particular interest, goal, or cause that motivates you to put in effort and stay committed even when faced with challenges. Passion fuels your determination and sustains your focus, making you more likely to achieve your objectives through hard work and persistence.

Two Great Reasons to Have a Passion

Discovering your passion is important, for two very compelling reasons. Firstly, a strong passion could help you steer clear of risky behaviors. When you're deeply engaged in a positive pursuit, you're less likely to get involved in activities like underage drinking, drugs, and other negative behaviors.

Secondly, it's important to note that colleges are increasingly interested in teens who showcase genuine passions. Most universities seek applicants who excel not only academically but also apply their academic skills in a real-world context. In the past, being a "well-rounded" student was highly regarded, but in today's competitive college landscape, top-ranked schools are searching for candidates who demonstrate focus and exceptional achievements in their chosen pursuits.

Possible Obstacles In Finding Your Passion

Apathy

Apathy is that sense of feeling nothing at all like it's hard to care about anything. It's a state of mind that can get worse if you ignore it. It often comes with other symptoms and can even be linked to nutritional issues. To tackle apathy, get to the root of what is causing it and face the hard questions you may be avoiding.

Fear

Fear might be at the heart of other problems like apathy and anxiety, and it's a tough one to overcome. The key is to recognize your fears, so you can confront and conquer them. Sometimes, facing your fears is the best way to make them go away.

The truth is that fear never really goes away. What changes is you. You can become stronger and more resilient by practicing all you have learned in this book. Try not to push fear away. Work with a therapist, try meditation, or get active in sports. Remember, you're never alone. Even if it's not your mom, your dad, or a friend, there's always someone you can turn to. Get support from someone you trust, but most importantly, trust yourself.

Anxiety

Anxiety is something we all feel. It's that worrying feeling you get about things that might happen in the future, and that uncertainty can really mess with your head. Anxiety disorders are generally complex and should best be handled by a specialist. But many teens, adults, and even kids deal with regular anxiety. Slay anxiety by getting out of your head and into your body! Physical activity of any kind, like yoga, swimming, or basketball can really help to move negative energy. It's also a good idea to take breaks from technology and get out into nature. Don't let these emotions hold you back from finding your passions.

How to Explore Your Passions

Make a List of All the Things That Make You Happy

Your passion might be hiding among these simple pleasures. Since passions are generally a source of happiness and satisfaction, your list could be the first piece of the puzzle. Afterwards, you can explore each item on your list uncovering hidden passions to dive deeper into.

Get Out of Your Comfort Zone

Passion often lies beyond the familiar. Think of your passion as a *person* who you must *meet*. You won't meet them by staying cuddled up in your comfort zone. Go out and expose yourself to new people, places, and experiences.

Talk to an Adult

Talking to an adult about your interests could help you feel more purpose-driven. Sometimes finding your passion isn't about igniting a flame, but about fanning a tiny spark already inside of you. Adults, when taking the role of mentors can become sources of inspiration, and it's their validation and concern that often ignites that spark.

Open Your Mind

Some teens have a hard time finding their passions because they think passion can only be a certain thing. For instance, if you come from a family of doctors and medical professionals, you might believe that is where your passion should lie. You may have preconceived ideas of what admirable and worthy passions are. Let go of all that. Listen to your inner voice and let it lead you to your passion.

Relax, and Avoid Stress

Finding your passion should be exciting and fun, not stressful. Stress will not help you, in fact, it will become an obstacle in your path to finding your passion. Trust that it will happen with time; passions are dynamic and they may change as you grow. You may discover new passions later in life, that you simply lack the life experience to unveil right now. You're at the threshold of adulthood, you're still becoming acquainted with yourself physically, mentally, and emotionally. While you strive to define who you are, it's normal to need time to find the answer to "What is your passion?"

Parents/Teacher: Assisting Your Teen in Discovering Their Passion

Support Their Interests

You might think, "Yeah, I don't forbid them from pursuing their interests," but the support we mean goes further than that. Teens require not only moral but also financial support to pursue their interests. As adults, it's important to actively facilitate their participation by ensuring they have the resources they need. To support your teen, you must allow them time to practice, permission to travel with their team, allowances for tools or material they might need, and words of motivation.

Find Your Teen a Mentor

Connect your teen with an expert in something closely related to their interests. Interacting with someone who's skilled in their area of interest will give your teen an idea of what's in store for them in the future. A mentor can highlight what your teen already knows and how much they still have to learn.

Encourage Your Teen to Develop Their Strengths

People often take their strengths for granted. As a parent or teacher, help your teen recognize the significance of their abilities by showing them the opportunities it could open up for them. For example, if your teen is articulate and loves to talk, have a chat with them about how to use this natural skill even more in their lives. Ask the following questions:

- How are you already using and benefiting from your natural strengths?
- What other areas of your life could benefit from using these same strengths?
- What activity could you take up or do more of that would help them develop these strengths?

ENCOURAGING YOUR CREATIVE SIDE

Benefits of Being Creative

Creativity is your capacity to think in fresh and unique ways. It's about finding novel solutions, coming up with original ideas, and expressing yourself in innovative ways. When you tap into your creativity, you can break free from the usual and discover exciting, out-of-the-box possibilities. Below we explore the benefits of fostering creativity in your life.

Cultivating creativity during your teenage years brings forth numerous advantages. Firstly, it serves as an effective stress reliever, enabling you to confront moments of anxiety with resilience. Furthermore, creativity provides an invaluable outlet for self-expression. When words fall short, your creative pursuits become your voice. Whether through painting, writing, or dancing, being creative helps you process your emotions in a healthy manner.

Nurturing your creativity also fosters resourcefulness. You'll discover innovative solutions to everyday challenges and enhance your problem-solving skills. As a result, creativity boosts your self-confidence, instilling a sense of empowerment that allows you to face any obstacle.

Moreover, creativity acts as a powerful motivator. Your creative ideas become a driving force, making school work more engaging and inspiring. You'll develop critical thinking abilities, connecting different academic disciplines that impress even your teachers. Furthermore, increased involvement in creative activities can lead to a significant boost to your overall happiness.

Five Ways to Cultivate Creativity

Cultivating your creativity can be a fun learning experience and you might be surprised by the talents you didn't know you had. Try out the five ideas below.

1. Claim your creative space: Find a place at home or at school that's your own for thinking and creating. It could be your desk, a corner with a comfy chair, or a special nook. Declare it as your creative zone, and let everyone know it's a place for inspiration to flow.
2. Visit your creative space: Make sure to use your creative space regularly, even when you don't feel particularly inspired. Just by being there, you invite

creative energy and ideas to emerge. Show up to your creative space consistently, and creativity will naturally start flowing.
3. Plan quiet moments: In our busy lives, finding time for stillness can be rare. Yet, these moments of silence can invite your inner creativity to flow. Only a few quiet minutes can spark more ideas than a full day of bustling distractions. Embrace stillness to clear your mind and create space for creative thoughts.
4. Be curious: Creativity is linked to curiosity. Ask questions, make mistakes, and seek new ways of doing things. Embrace curiosity in your projects, problem-solving, and leadership. Being curious helps you seek new information that will expand your perception.
5. Engage in storytelling: Stories are a powerful tool for sparking creativity. You have your own unique experiences and a story to tell. Sharing your journey and hearing others' stories can inspire creativity within you. Share your experiences and encourage your friends to do the same.

Parents/Teachers: How to Raise a Creative Teen

Identify your teen's unique gifts and passions by observing what brings them joy and where they excel. Whether it's music, athletics, art, or craftsmanship, these gifts are essential to your teen's path in life. Shine a light on their talents and encourage your teen to explore and develop them.

Cultivate creativity at home by surrounding your family with inspiring literature, poetry, and music. Introduce them to the world of art through books, posters, or prints. Teach them practical creative skills like cooking, gardening, or crafting. Although you might not engage in every creative endeavor with your teenager, the ones you do explore together can serve as building blocks that pave the way for others.

Share your favorite creative pursuits with your teen. Pass on your favorite music, books, or art, and don't forget to explain why you appreciate them. By sharing your passions, you create a connection and inspire creative pursuits in your teen.

Allow self-expression in their appearance. Let your teens express themselves through clothing and hairstyles, even if you don't approve of their choices. It's a way for them to assert their individuality and creativity.

Never ridicule or reject your teen for their creative expression. Embrace the missteps they are bound to make and offer constructive feedback to encourage their growth. Ensure they understand their significance, both as individuals and in the realm of artistic expression.

Practical Tool: Passion-Discovery Activities

If you're a teen looking to explore your interests and talents, there's a wide range of activities that might align with your unique qualities:

- Outdoor adventures: If you're energetic and love exploring, activities like hiking, biking, walking, and climbing can be perfect. They allow you to stay active without the bustle of being in a team, which is great if you prefer solitude.
- Musical pursuits: If you have a passion for music and singing, you'll enjoy exploring the world of melodies and rhythm. Learning to play an instrument is a fantastic way to explore music. You can also consider joining a group like a band, or try mixing your own beats as a DJ.
- Debate club: For those who enjoy sharing their knowledge and thoughts, debate can be a valuable option. It's a chance to unleash your competitive side, while enhancing your communication skills, connecting with like-minded peers, and learning effective organization of ideas.
- Drama: If storytelling is your forte, drama club offers an outlet for your creativity. You'll discover how elements like plot, characters, and setting work together to craft a compelling story. There are also behind-the-scenes roles for those who prefer to work as part of a team, such as set design and costumes.
- Coding: If you are fascinated by computers and how they work, you'll find coding to be the perfect field to explore. You can explore coding on your own through online resources or join classes. Coding hones your problem-solving skills, flexible thinking, and attention to detail.

IN SUMMARY

Your teenage years are a crucial time to define your passion and cultivate your creativity. Passion is about finding what truly excites you, often hidden within your everyday interests. You can uncover your passions by stepping out of your comfort zone, engaging in open-minded exploration, listing what makes you happy, and seeking guidance from adults.

Creativity, meanwhile, serves as a powerful tool for stress reduction, self-expression, and skill development. Mentors can be valuable allies who offer you opportunities to explore, provide a safe space for self-expression, and nurture your creativity. While you're still brimming with passion and creativity, go on to the final chapter where we focus on facing fears and overcoming insecurities.

9

CLAPBACK ON THOSE FEARS: FACING FEARS AND OVERCOMING INSECURITIES

> *The reason we struggle with insecurity is because we compare our behind-the-scenes with everyone else's highlight reel.*
>
> — STEVE FURTICK

TEEN STORY OF COURAGE

One summer evening, 16-year-old James York and his father spotted their neighbor's house on fire while they were outside doing some yard work. They rushed to the scene and found most family members outside, but found out 7-year-old Cameron was still trapped on the second floor. James' father initially attempted the rescue, but when the intense heat and smoke forced him out, James fearlessly took matters into his own hands.

James used the ladder they had been using to clean out the gutters and positioned it beneath the second-story window. With his father steadying the ladder, James opened the window and helped him get out safely. Though Cameron had to go to the hospital, he was ultimately unharmed. Despite being hailed as a hero by the community, 16-year-old James remains humble, stating, "I can't say I really consider myself a hero... I think anyone would have done what I did."

UNDERSTANDING YOUR FEARS AND INSECURITIES

Insecurities are those nagging doubts and worries you might have about yourself—specifically your appearance, abilities, or possessions. They can make you question your worth, whether you fit in, or if you're good enough at something. Insecurities often stem from comparing yourself to others, feeling different, or being afraid of judgment. While everyone feels insecure at times, your insecurities don't define your value or potential. Recognizing and understanding your insecurities is the first step to managing and overcoming them, helping you grow with confidence.

Types of Insecurities

Navigating your teenage years means encountering a multitude of insecurities stemming from the world around you. Social insecurities come from the pressures of fitting in and making friends, or the fear of being judged by your peers for your choices. Negative peer pressure, a major cause of social insecurities, can lead to self-doubt, as you might feel compelled to conform to what your friends are doing, even if it doesn't align with your values. For instance, you may feel pressured to try alcohol at a party because everyone else is, but deep down, you know it's not the right choice for you. Learning how to cope with peer pressure is about striking the right balance between being yourself and fitting in with your friends.

Another common insecurity relates to body image. In today's world of filters and Photoshop, you might find yourself comparing your appearance to the highly edited images you see on social media. This can cause you to feel dissatisfied with your body and appearance, even though those images often represent an unrealistic standard. Always remember that your true value goes beyond your physical appearance.

Family-related insecurities can also arise from the dynamics at home. Perhaps you don't feel understood or supported by your family, which can lead to feelings of isolation and self-doubt. Family issues, such as divorce or conflict, can further worsen these insecurities.

Lastly, insecurities caused by traumatic events can be deeply unsettling. Whether you've experienced bullying, abuse, or a significant loss, these events can leave emotional scars that make you question your worth and shake your confidence. It's important to remember that these insecurities are common, and there are ways to overcome them.

Parents/Teachers: Recognizing Signs of Teen Insecurity

Keep an eye out for the following signs of insecurity in your teen:

- Loose or baggy clothes: If your teen suddenly seems to favor loose or baggy clothing, they may have body image insecurities they are trying to hide. For instance, if your teen regularly wore skinny jeans, shorts, and skirts but now suddenly wears oversized t-shirts, baggy pants, loose dresses, etc.
- Isolation from friends: If your teen seems to avoid spending time with their friends, they may be dealing with social anxiety or feelings of inadequacy. For example, if they seem to prefer to stay home instead of going out with their group, attending parties, or engaging in other social activities they previously enjoyed.
- Self-deprecating comments: Teens who frequently make self-deprecating comments might struggle with confidence in their abilities. Your teen might make these comments in a fairly cheerful manner, masking it as a joke. However, self-deprecating comments, even those made in a humorous way, often stem from real insecurities. For instance, if your teen says things like, "I'm an expert at failing," or "I'm the human equivalent of a typo," too often, they might be battling low self-esteem and self-doubt.
- Hesitancy to voice opinions: Teens who rarely express their opinions may feel unimportant or unheard. For

example, if your teen avoids speaking up during family discussions or with their peers, it could be due to a fear of being dismissed or ridiculed.
- Constantly seeking validation: If your teen constantly fishes for compliments or asks for everyone's opinions, it could indicate that they feel doubtful about their own thoughts or actions. For example, they might frequently post pictures on social media, seeking validation through likes and comments. This behavior may stem from a lack of certainty in their identity and the need for external reassurance.

Parents/Teachers: Guidance for Empowering Your Teen to Conquer Insecurities

Be Supportive

Make it clear that you expect to be the first person your teen turns to for help, and ensure you create an atmosphere where they feel comfortable doing so. By actively listening to their worries while trying to understand their perspective, and by offering encouragement, practical advice, and reassurance, you instill confidence that they can confide in you without fear of judgment.

Another way of showing support is to avoid being unnecessarily harsh. Excessive criticism over minor matters can discourage your teen from sharing their worries because they could be afraid that you might overreact or get angry. If you need to reprimand your teen, a more effective strategy is to wait until you've calmed down.

Know Their Triggers

Where do your teen's insecurities stem from? Whether it's their body image, social interactions, or the effects of trauma, knowing what lies at the root of the problem will help you deal with the cause and not merely focus on the symptoms. Think of the times when an interaction with your teen led to conflict. What triggers may *you* have that cause you to react negatively resulting in conflict? Identify those too, to help foster open and effective communication between you and your teen.

Help Them Set Goals

When your teen is in a bad space and dealing with issues such as insecurities, anxiety, or depression, not having a clear goal in mind, or a plan for the future can make you feel like now is the only reality there will ever be. Helping your teen set goals and make clear plans for the future will make them see what they're going through today is simply a chapter in their life story. Furthermore, breaking goals down into smaller steps, and achieving them one at a time builds self-confidence.

Establish Structures

Structure in your teen's life provides a sense of stability and comfort, especially during times of emotional turmoil. Having a reliable routine can offer predictability in the midst of chaos. It doesn't have to be very rigid, but ensure there is some aspect of their day that is predictable to bring about a sense of certainty. One example is to establish a 6:30 p.m. family dinner at the table every night, with no phones.

CONFRONTING FEAR HEAD-ON

What Is Fear?

Fear is one of the most fundamental human emotions. It's hardwired into our nervous system and operates as an instinct. Right from infancy, we come equipped with the survival instincts to respond with fear when we detect danger or feel unsafe.

Fear serves as a protective mechanism. It keeps us vigilant to potential threats and prepares us to confront them. Experiencing fear is entirely natural and, in certain circumstances, highly beneficial. Fear can act as an alert, a signal that advises us to exercise caution.

Similar to all our emotions, fear can range from mild to intense, varying based on the situation and the individual. Feelings of fear can be fleeting or prolonged, depending on the circumstances.

Common Fears You May Experience

Fear of Failure

You're no stranger to this one, and who can blame you? You're under constant pressure to succeed. You know good grades are the ticket to getting into a "good" college, which seems like the key to a "good" life. Thoughts of not getting into college, failing at college, or at work can rob you of your peace. When it feels like your entire future is on the line, the fear of messing things up is completely natural.

Fear of the Unknown

Being afraid of uncertainty is particularly understandable during your teenage years. You're at the gateway of adulthood and you wonder what lies in store for you. The prospect of moving out and becoming independent, changing schools, choosing a career path, or making new friends can be incredibly intimidating.

Fear of Being a Disappointment

No teen wants to disappoint their parents, let down their friends, or miss that game-winning shot for their team. If you have parents who expect excellent grades, teachers who have high expectations, or teammates who see you as their 'secret weapon', you could experience this fear more intensely than others. There could be real consequences if you push yourself too hard to make others happy instead of nurturing your own self-confidence.

Fear of Rejection

Imagine it's one week to the prom, and nobody's asked you to be their date. Or you're home on a Saturday night, idly scrolling through your feed until you see a live-stream video of your friends enjoying a night out, *without you*. Rejection feels terrible, no matter the context. Being accepted and loved is so important to you, as it is to many teens, and anything that threatens that acceptance can be really scary.

Fear of Embarrassment

In the teenage world where social status is everything, embarrassment, or anything that might hurt your social reputation, is terrifying. Make one wrong move, and it becomes a viral video, documented forever. Say the wrong thing, and you're shunned by the popular crowd. Embarrass yourself on a date, and you think you'll probably be single forever. With stakes this high, it's no wonder you may genuinely fear embarrassment.

How to Face Your Fears Head-On

You have fears, but so do most people. Life doesn't come to a standstill because you're scared, it goes on regardless. It's important that you rise above fear and experience life from a place of assurance, peace of mind, and resilience. Below we explore a number of ways you can overcome your fears.

Calm Down

Fear tends to terrorize us before anything even happens. Have you ever found yourself overthinking about a mortifying situation that is unlikely to ever happen to you? Just the thought of our fears can bring about very real emotions of panic. In these situations, the first step is to calm yourself down. Do some breathing exercises that force you to focus your mind on slowing your breathing, gradually your heart rate will drop and you'll feel better.

Think Logically

While you're calm, think about your fears logically. Consider all the factors and the likelihood of your fear ever materializing. Draw upon your knowledge of past events, statistics, and your best judgment. Take your fear of not making or keeping friends, as an example. From kindergarten, up until today, how many friends have you made? Having just one friend already discredits your fear, but go on to ask yourself, "What logical reason is there that would explain why I won't make any new friends, ever again?" When looking at your fears objectively, you'll realize how much you've exaggerated the risks.

Practice Positive Self-Talk

Positive self-talk enhances your confidence, fosters self-compassion, and reduces stress. These benefits collectively empower you to conquer your fears. Consider a scenario where you're facing an upcoming class presentation. On the night before the presentation, practice positive self-talk and tell yourself, "Although I might not feel fully prepared, I know that I am. I acknowledge my fear, but I know it is irrational. I am confident in the preparation I've done. Tomorrow, my performance will be excellent, and I can't wait to embrace it as a valuable learning experience."

Stop Judging Yourself

Imagine trying to confront and overcome your fears while being burdened by self-criticism for having those fears in the first place. Judging yourself for having fears will cause you unnecessary strain and stress, because as we said earlier fear is a normal part of life. So, instead of looking down on yourself for having fears, focus on facing them and eventually overcoming them. After all, you're just as human as everyone else, and you deserve to receive love, patience, and encouragement from yourself.

Talk to a Counselor

Sometimes we allow our fears to fester to the extent that they become too powerful for us to control on our own. In this case, seek professional help. Talking to a counselor is not only effective but also a great testament to your commitment to self-care and growth. You may be able to access a counselor at school, at church, or in your community.

Parents/Teacher: How To Help Your Teen Overcome Their Fears

Communication

Establishing open communication with your teen is a crucial step in helping them confront their fears. Create an environment where your teen feels comfortable discussing their fears and concerns. Engage in honest conversations about their feelings, explore the potential impacts on their life, and actively listen to gain insight into their perspective.

Empathy

Teenagers often experience fear in isolation, believing that they are alone in their struggles. This sense of isolation can lead to shame. Expressing empathy for your teen not only provides them with reassurance but also strengthens your connection.

Let your teen know that you understand their fears, support them, and take their concerns seriously to help foster a sense of security and trust.

Independence

While your parental instinct may be to shield your teen from fear and its sources, it's crucial to encourage independence, especially during their adolescent years. Providing solutions for every problem can hinder their ability to cope with fear independently. Instead, help them realize their capacity to face fear and even encounter failures. These experiences promote resilience and independence, equipping them with valuable skills for addressing various challenges throughout life.

Practical Tool: Overcoming Fear and Insecurity

Good self-esteem is helpful in overcoming insecurities and fears. Below is an easy exercise to help you work on building solid self-esteem.

Instructions:

- Positive self-talk: Write down three positive affirmations about yourself. For example, "I am capable," "I am unique," "I can overcome challenges."
- Strengths inventory: List five things you are good at or proud of. It could be a hobby, a skill, or a personal quality.

- Past successes: Recall three times when you achieved something or overcame a challenge. Describe what you accomplished and how it made you feel.
- Growth goals: Identify one area you'd like to improve. It could be related to your fears or insecurities. Write down a specific, achievable goal for this area.
- Support system: List three people who support you and make you feel good about yourself. Consider why they support you.
- Affirming self-compassion: Write a kind message to yourself as if you were comforting a friend who is feeling down.

IN SUMMARY

In this chapter, we unpacked two sensitive issues: insecurities and fears. You learned what they are, the different types of insecurities and fears, and how you, with the help of parents and teachers, can overcome them. It's important to remember that everyone, from all walks of life and life stages, experiences the negative consequences of insecurities and fears. By calming down, thinking logically, using positive self-talk, and talking to a trusted mentor, you can effectively face your fears.

CONCLUSION

As we conclude this empowering journey, you've embarked on an incredible quest to overthrow the negativity that's been holding you back. Your transformation is nothing short of a *Teen Confidence Revolution,* and you've come a long way in discovering how to navigate through the often tumultuous teenage years. Let's wrap up our journey together by revisiting the heart of what you've learned throughout this book.

Create a mental toolkit for yourself so that at any time, you can pull out the inspiration you need to keep the revolution going. First, always remember that you have the power to transform your life by building confidence, managing stress, and setting and achieving meaningful goals. For challenges and negativity that are unhealthy and overtake your capacity to believe in yourself you have the tools of self-belief and resilience. To improve your mental and emotional well-being, leading to a happier and more successful adolescence, you have the practical techniques and activities shared in this book that you can do as often as you need.

No longer do you have to grapple with questions of identity, purpose, and self-discovery as the tools of positive self-talk and self-awareness give you the courage to take on challenging tasks. You now know how to best deal with stress, anxiety, depression, and feelings of isolation and that setting meaningful goals can give you a sense of direction and motivation.

Along this journey, you have also identified and created connections to a supportive and uplifting community of people who will cheer you on! Affirm to yourself, write it across the pages of your journal, or share it with a trusted friend… you are to be celebrated!

Your *Teen Confidence Revolution* ultimately confirms the following: You are capable of greatness, and your unique qualities are your superpowers. You don't need to fit into someone else's mold because your uniqueness is your strength. Self-compassion and confidence will guide you on your path to success. As you close this book and move forward, remember that your journey is far from over.

You've laid the foundation now, it's time to take the reins and continue to practice and live the strategies within this book. You are a success story in the making. The future holds incredible opportunities, and you have the power to shape your own destiny. Your potential and your ability to overcome challenges is limitless.

If this book has been a source of inspiration and transformation for you, consider leaving a review. Share your journey with others who may be seeking guidance on their path to instilling a sense of confidence and resilience in themselves. By sharing your experiences, you can become a source of inspiration for someone else's *Teen Confidence Revolution*.

And one more thing about your revolution—it's not forced. It happens naturally, focusing on what's going on in your world and what you can control. Sure, your revolution might have the power to change the whole world, but it starts with what you can do right now.

So, think about all you've learned. Dig deep and find that inner awareness that shows you the unique quality you bring to this world. Continue your confidence revolution and bust out of the mold of being like everyone else. You'll be amazed at what you discover about yourself!

PASSING THE TORCH
YOUR REVIEW MATTERS

Now that you've equipped yourself with the tools to crush negativity, boost self-esteem, reduce stress, and slay your goals, it's time to share the wealth of knowledge. By leaving your honest opinion on Amazon, you're not just reviewing a book; you're guiding fellow teen readers to the source of valuable information and igniting their passion for pursuing their own ***Teen Confidence Revolution.***

Your help is invaluable in keeping the flame of self-discovery alive as we pass on our knowledge. Thank you for being part of this journey and contributing to the positive change we aim to create.

Warm regards,

Teen Powerhouse Society

REFERENCES

Alisha. (2017, November 5). *100 Quotes on Art & Creativity*. Masterpiece Society. https://masterpiecesociety.com/100-quotes-art-creativity/

Association for Psychological Science. (2017, July 17). *Asking Questions Increases Likability*. https://www.psychologicalscience.org/news/minds-business/asking-questions-increases-likability.html

At Risk Youth Programs. (2023, March 31). *Build Confidence & Overcoming Low Self-Esteem in Teenagers*. https://atriskyouthprograms.com/low-self-esteem-in-teenagers-2/

Beautifully Simply You. (2019, February 4). *Celebrate Your Uniqueness*. https://beautifullysimplyyou.com/2019/02/04/celebrate-your-uniqueness/

Blount, S. (2019, March 2). *Three Ways To Grow From Failure*. Forbes. https://www.forbes.com/sites/sallyblount/2019/05/02/three-ways-to-grow-from-failure/?sh=73cc72b5666d

Brundin, J. (2019, December 2). *Teen Diary: Amelia Tells Us How Academic Stress Led Her To A Breakdown*. Colorado Public Radio. https://www.cpr.org/2019/12/02/teen-diary-amelia-tells-us-how-academic-stress-led-her-to-a-breakdown/

Castrillon, C. (2020, November 24). *How To Stop Comparing Yourself To Others*. Forbes. https://www.forbes.com/sites/carolinecastrillon/2020/11/24/how-to-stop-comparing-yourself-to-others/?sh=7fc8b88c6473

Deane, J. (2021, December 16). *How To Reflect On The Past Year And Set Goals For The Year Ahead*. LinkedIn. https://www.linkedin.com/pulse/how-reflect-past-year-set-goals-ahead-jennifer-deane-pcc-she-her-/

Derr, A. (2020, October 16). *Social Connection Quotes*. Visible Network Labs. https://visiblenetworklabs.com/2020/10/16/thirty-three-best-social-connection-quotes/

Difference Psychology. (2022, August 19). *WOOP!* https://differencepsychology.com.au/newsletters/f/woop

Eatough, E. (2022, January 7). *How to say no to others (and why you shouldn't feel guilty)*. BetterUp. https://www.betterup.com/blog/how-to-say-no

Eatough, E. (2023, October 5). *"We are the champions" plus other qualities every good friend should have*. BetterUp. https://www.forbes.com/sites/sallyblount/2019/05/02/three-ways-to-grow-from-failure/?sh=73cc72b5666d

Emerson, M. (2023, February 6). *8 Tips For Better Communication Skills*. Forbes. https://www.forbes.com/sites/harvard-division-of-continuing-education/2023/02/06/8-tips-for-better-communication-skills/?sh=7ec7e93a6993

Erieau, C. (2019, February 20). *The 50 best resilience quotes*. Hello Driven. https://home.hellodriven.com/articles/the-50-best-resilience-quotes/

Families for Life. (n.d.). *How to Strengthen Your Extended Family Ties*. https://ffl.familiesforlife.sg/pages/Article/How-to-Strengthen-Your-Extended-Family-Ties

Graham, L. (2016, September 16). *4 Ways to Find Your Unique Voice*. Thrive Global. https://community.thriveglobal.com/4-ways-to-find-your-unique-voice/

Hailey, L. (n.d.). *How to Set Boundaries: 5 Ways to Draw the Line Politely*. Science of People. https://www.scienceofpeople.com/how-to-set-boundaries/

Hansen, L. (2015, January 9). *9 heroic teens and their incredible acts of bravery [Updated]*. The Week. https://theweek.com/articles/468498/9-heroic-teens-incredible-acts-bravery-updated

Health Direct. (2022, July). *Motivation: How to get started and staying motivated*. https://www.healthdirect.gov.au/motivation-how-to-get-started-and-staying-motivated

Heather. (2019, November 30). *The Importance of Connection for Adolescents*. Heather Hayes & Associates. https://www.heatherhayes.com/the-importance-of-connection-for-adolescents/

Heckman, W. (2017). *6 Common Triggers of Teen Stress*. The American Institute of Stress. https://www.stress.org/6-common-triggers-of-teen-stress

Hill, J. (2023, August 18). *14 Reasons To Always Try New Things in Life*. LifeHack. https://www.lifehack.org/902478/try-new-things

Hundley, S. (2020, October 22). *How to Make Time for More Fun!* Mindful Counseling. https://mindfulcounselingutah.com/blog/2020/10/22/how-to-make-time-for-more-fun/

Hurley, K. (2022, June 14). *What Is Resilience? Definition, Types, Building Resiliency, Benefits, and Resources*. EverydayHealth.com. https://www.everydayhealth.com/wellness/resilience/

Kaminsky, A. (2016, September 16). *Teens, Social Media And The Illusion Of Perfection*. Pys-Ed. https://www.psy-ed.com/wpblog/teens-and-social-media/

Kristenson, S. (2022a, May 19). *11 Benefits of Developing a Growth Mindset in Life*. Develop Good Habits. https://www.developgoodhabits.com/benefits-growth-mindset/

Kristenson, S. (2022b, June 2). *7 Proven Alternatives to SMART Goals*. Develop Good Habits. https://www.developgoodhabits.com/smart-goals-alternative/

Latham, G., & Locke, E. (2007). New Developments in and Directions for Goal-Setting Research. *European Psychologist 12*(4):290-300 https://www.researchgate.net/publication/247399303_New_Developments_in_and_Directions_for_Goal-Setting_Research

Lauren. (2022, May 30). *100 Powerful Self Confidence Quotes for Girls*. Simply Well Balanced. https://simply-well-balanced.com/confidence-quotes-for-girls/

Legg, T. (2021, January 27). *Gut Feelings Are Real, but Should You Really "Trust Your Gut"?* Healthline. https://www.healthline.com/health/mental-health/trust-your-gut

Machina, Z. (2022). *5 Dangers of Having a Fixed Mindset*. PHASE. https://phase.undock.com/5-dangers-of-having-a-fixed-mindset/

Madill, E. (n.d.). *How to Transform Challenges into Opportunities for Growth*. Vunela. https://www.vunela.com/how-to-transform-challenges-into-opportunities-for-growth/

Magana, S., Morrow, D., Bird, M., Toribio, Y., & Khan, H. (2017). *Student Success Stories*. Student Success at The University of Utah. https://studentsuccess.utah.edu/advocates/student-success-stories/

Martinez, N. (2023, March 7). *5 Reasons You Should Unplug From Social Media*. CNET. https://www.cnet.com/health/mental/unplug-from-social-media/

May, L. (2023, September 7). *Is confidence inherited or a learned skill?* LinkedIn. https://www.linkedin.com/pulse/confidence-inherited-learned-skill-lisa-may-gaicd

Moore, C. (2019, March 4). *Positive Daily Affirmations: Is There Science Behind It?* Positive Psychology. https://positivepsychology.com/daily-affirmations/#research

MyMnCareers. (n.d.). *Long-Term and Short-Term Goals*. https://careerwise.minnstate.edu/mymncareers/finish-school/long-short-goals.html

Parenting Teens and Tweens. (2023, May 31). *24 Inspiring Quotes to Help Your Anxious Teenager*. https://parentingteensandtweens.com/best-quotes-for-anxious-teens/

Patel, S. (2020, June 19). *The 12 Morning Rituals That Help to Kick Off Successful*

Days. The Muse. https://www.themuse.com/advice/the-12-morning-rituals-that-help-to-kick-off-successful-days

Pederson, T. (2023, February 27). *How Does Social Media Affect Body Image?* PsychCentral. https://psychcentral.com/health/how-the-media-affects-body-image

Price-Mitchell, M. (2018, June 26). *Self-Awareness Quotes That Help Kids Explore Their Inner Selves*. Roots of Action. https://www.rootsofaction.com/self-awareness-quotes/

Putman, P., Antypa, N., Crysovergi, P., & van der Does, W. A. J. (2009). Exogenous cortisol acutely influences motivated decision making in healthy young men. *Psychopharmacology, 208*(2), 257–263. https://doi.org/10.1007/s00213-009-1725-y

Raising Healthy Teens. (2019, December 31). *Tips to Help Your Teen Cultivate Their Passion*. https://raisinghealthyteens.org/tips-to-help-your-teen-cultivate-their-passion/

ReachOut. (n.d.). *Stress and teenagers*. https://parents.au.reachout.com/common-concerns/everyday-issues/stress-and-teenagers

Restless Development. (2020, August 11). *Four stories of youth resilience from around the world*. https://restlessdevelopment.org/2020/08/four-stories-of-youth-resilience-from-around-the-world/

Richardson, T. (2020, September 18). *6 Actionable Ways To Find & Speak Your Truth*. Mind Body Green. https://www.mindbodygreen.com/articles/how-to-find-and-speak-your-truth

Rood, E. (2020, October 13). *Building Self-Awareness and Emotional Intelligence in Teens*. Inspire Balance. https://www.inspirebalance.com/eq-self-awareness-teens/

Rusack, P. (2023, January 4). *69 Inspirational Goal-Setting Quotes*. We Are Teachers. https://www.weareteachers.com/goal-setting-quotes/

Sabrina. (2023, October 27). *7 Quotes about Insecurity for Teens*. All Womens Talk. https://teen.allwomenstalk.com/quotes-about-insecurity-for-teens/

Salameh, S. (2023, May 24). *Young dreamers making a difference in their communities*. UNICEF. https://www.unicef.org/syria/stories/young-dreamers-making-difference-their-communities

Self Esteem School. (n.d.). *Some Interesting Self Esteem Statistics and Fact You Might Not Be Aware Of*. https://www.self-esteem-school.com/self-esteem-statistics.html

Shonk, K. (2023, July 31). *What is Conflict Resolution, and How Does It Work?*

REFERENCES | 169

Program on Negotiation; Harvard Law School. https://www.pon.harvard.edu/daily/conflict-resolution/what-is-conflict-resolution-and-how-does-it-work/

Slumber Kins. (2020, February 28). *One in 7.7 Billion: Raising Children to be Their Authentic Self.* https://slumberkins.com/blogs/slumberkins-blog/one-in-7-7-billion

Smamore Castle. (2023, July 4). *12 Ways to Overcome Your Mindless Scrolling Habit.* https://www.smarmore-rehab-clinic.com/blog/addiction-advice/12-ways-to-overcome-your-mindless-scrolling-habit/

StopBullying. (2019, September 24). *Facts about bullying.* Department of Health and Human Services. https://www.stopbullying.gov/resources/facts

Thomas, T. (2023, July 20). *Embracing My Unique Difference: A Journey as a Dextrocardian.* Medium. https://medium.com/@theretaleacademy/embracing-my-unique-difference-a-journey-as-a-dextrocardian-b919279bf65dT

Victoria University. (n.d.). *How to make an effective study plan.* Victoria University Melbourne Australia. https://www.vu.edu.au/about-vu/news-events/study-space/how-to-make-an-effective-study-plan

Vogt, C. (2021, September 1). *Under Pressure: Are the Stresses of Social Media Too Much for Teens and Young Adults?* Everyday Health. https://www.everydayhealth.com/emotional-health/under-pressure/are-the-stresses-of-social-media-too-much-for-teens-and-young-adults/

Walsh, E. (2022, October 27). *Teens and Screens: Why The Shift From Control to Connection is Key to Mental Health.* Spark & Stitch Institute. https://sparkandstitchinstitute.com/teens-and-screens-why-the-shift-from-control-to-connection-is-key-to-mental-health/

Wilding, M. (2021, December 13). *5 Myths About Confidence That Are Making You More Insecure.* Forbes. https://www.forbes.com/sites/melodywilding/2021/12/13/5-myths-about-confidence-that-are-making-you-more-insecure/?sh=4e2eeca7bbf1

Williams, J. (2018, September 4). *Developing Adolescent Identity.* Parent and Teen. https://parentandteen.com/developing-adolescent-identity/

Wisal, K. (2019, October 15). *Insecurities Among Teenagers.* Medium. https://medium.com/@kashifawisal786/insecurities-among-teenagers-2f40631e53ba